THE BURNING JUNGLE:

An Analysis of Arthur Miller's *Death of a Salesman*

Karl Harshbarger

University Press of America™

This book is for R W and L B

TABLE OF CONTENTS

INTRODUCTION

At 8:15 of the morning after <u>Death of a Salesman</u> opened
in New York City a line began to form at the ticket window of
the Morosco Theatre. By the time that window opened an hour
and forty-five minutes later the line stretched down the
street to the Music Box Theatre. The reason for this activity
so early in the morning was that Miller's new play had been
met, according to the <u>New York Herald Tribune</u>, "with an acclaim
such as Broadway has not seen in years" [1949, p. 9]. Some
indication of the audience's initial reaction can be gaged by
the effusiveness of the popular reviewers. Brooks Atkinson
of <u>The New York Times</u> wrote that it "is one of the finest
dramas in the whole range of American theatre" [1949, p. 27],
Wolcott Gibbs of <u>The New Yorker</u> commented that the play is a
"tremendously affecting work" [1949, p. 54], and Howard Barnes
of <u>The New York Herald Tribune</u> called it a "searing tragedy"
with "shattering dramatic impact" [1949, p. 14]. Probably
the most enthusiastic review came from John Mason Brown of
<u>The Saturday Review of Literature</u>.

> How good the writing of this or that of Mr.
> Miller's individual scenes may be, I do not
> know. Nor do I really care. When hit in
> the face, you do not bother to count all the
> knuckles which strike you. All that matters,
> all you remember, is the staggering impact
> of the blow. Mr. Miller's is a terrific
> wallop, as furious in its onslaught on the
> heart as on the head. The play is the most
> poignant statement of man as he must face
> himself to have come out of our theatre [1949,
> p. 30].

While some latitude, of course, must be allowed for the
conditions of an opening night, these judgments seem essentially
correct: <u>Death of a Salesman</u> has continued through the years
to have an overwhelming impact on most who see it. The play
is admitted to be one of the masterpieces of the American
theatre. Hayman, for one, can call the play "the best American play ever written" [1970, p. 27]; and even Hynes, who has
written a brilliantly damning piece on <u>Death of a Salesman</u>, can
agree "there would be no occasion for my remarks but for the
undeniable power which has made the play a theatrical

1

triumph. . ." [1963, p. 574].

In a natural and inevitable attempt to do justice to the play, two streams of criticism have evolved over the years. One group of critics attribute the power of Death of a Salesman primarily to Miller's social criticism. Certainly the authoritative and effective social observation is striking. Yet one need only compare Death of a Salesman with the cultural and political specificity of many of Miller's other plays to understand that his real concern here is elsewhere. Though vaguely identified as living in Brooklyn, the Lomans talk in such a strange abstract way as to defy an analysis of their ethnic background. World War II is barely mentioned, and unbelievably, there is no reference at all, direct or indirect, to the Great Depression. If the play is an attack on the American business system, the attack is curiously confused. The two most decent characters, Charlie and the adult Bernard, function as part of the capitalist way of life. If anything, the social message inherent in the play seems to be: study hard and you'll end up arguing before the Supreme Court and playing tennis at a friend's private court.

The other group of critics, correctly, in my opinion, find the power of the play to reside not in its descriptions of an ailing society but in Miller's portrayal of the human condition. (Indeed, many think that Miller has successfully created a universal tragedy--modernized, of course.) The paths and byways of this stream of criticism are so extensive and contradictory that any attempt at a summary of them here would be of little value. Suffice it to say that these arguments have done more to bear witness to the power of the play than to seek out the source of that power. Critics have yet to understand the depth and intensity of the characterizations of Willy, Linda, Biff and Happy; yet it is this very depth and intensity which account for the overwhelming impact of the play. The Lomans are so familiar to us, so readily recognizable and identifiable, that we can too easily ignore the rich and precise portrayal of the underlying passions within the family.

This study centers on those underlying passions. Such an examination involves a detailed consideration of the contradictions in behavior by which each character reveals himself; through this revelation of their inner reality the figures of the play emerge as something more than familiar stereotypes and grip us as complex, and at times appalling reflections of our deeper human selves.

I am grateful to a number of people who at various stages of the development of this manuscript have given me invaluable suggestions: James Knapp, Philip Wion, Kate White, Susan Evans, Susan Wall, James Kissane, Peter Connelly and Michael Cavanagh.

Karl Harshbarger

St. Mary's College of Maryland

Chapter I

LINDA

I

The critical commentary on <u>Death of a Salesman</u> is quite
naturally directed at Willy and Biff. While writers have not
ignored Linda, she is not considered central to the tragic
action of the play. The strength and tenacity of her love for
Willy and her determination to hold her family together appear
to be in reassuring contrast to those around her. She seems
to represent the older values of decency, courage, self-
sacrifice, and devotion. She has taken a difficult path and
has held to it. Indeed, it is possible to suggest that part
of the power of the play can be found not in the way other
members of the family tear each other apart, but in the way
Linda attempts to hold them together.[1] It is not accidental
that almost invariably in critical discussions of Linda's
character, writers quote her "Attention, attention must
finally be paid" speech, for these lines epitomize her devotion to decency in human relationships.[2] To my knowledge all
actresses who have successfully created Linda have portrayed
her as the loving, supporting, all-patient wife (and I have
centrally in mind Mildred Dunnock's original creation).[3] And,
indeed, Miller in describing her character in the stage
directions tells us: "<u>she more than loves him</u> [Willy]."

This quote from the stage directions is taken out of context from a much longer description of Linda's character, and
it is important to put it back into context:

<u>Most often jovial, she has developed an</u>
<u>iron repression of her exceptions to Willy's</u>
<u>behavior--she more than loves him, she</u>
<u>admires him, as though his mercurial nature,</u>
<u>his temper, his massive dreams and little</u>
<u>cruelties, served her only as sharp reminders</u>
<u>of the turbulent longings within him, long-</u>
<u>ings which she shares but lacks the temperament</u>

5

            to utter and follow to their end.

The most striking characteristic that Miller describes in Linda
is that she is "Most often jovial"--striking because that is the
one characteristic she hardly ever displays. No one on seeing
the play would think of describing her dominant mood as jovial.
We have only Miller's word that this is her natural state. What
is much more obvious is the attitude Miller explains that she
has developed: "an iron repression." There is a quality of
denial around Linda. She holds her own longings and feelings
within her. She may have once been most often jovial, but
certainly no longer.

     Miller's description of Linda--quoted above--is divided
into two parts. In the first Miller suggests she was once
jovial but has developed an iron repression, and in the second
(after the dash) he suggests the dynamics of that repression.
It is true that "she more than loves him." But this should not
be taken to mean that her love for Willy is more powerful than
most loves--a sort of super-love. Love is a giving, freeing
emotion, and clearly the qualities of love, on the one hand,
and iron repression, on the other, do not go together. Rather
what Miller emphasizes is not her love but her admiration. And
clearly she doesn't admire Willy for what he is now (she has
already developed an "iron repression of her exceptions to
Willy's behavior"), but rather for what he might have been. All
the oddities in his personality ("his mercurial nature, his
temper, his massive dreams and little cruelties") serve "her
only as sharp reminders of the turbulent longings within
him. . . ." Willy is an incomplete person, someone who has
never been able to fulfill his inner needs, never been able to
achieve his "turbulent longings." It is this potential, now
lost, she admires. Furthermore, Miller makes it clear that her
feelings are more than admiration. Her admiration is a form of
identification. The oddities in his personality

               served her only as sharp reminders of the
               turbulent longings within him, longings
               which she shares but lacks the temperament
               to utter and follow to their end.

Her admiration of Willy's potential is finally a vehicle for
finding expression of her own longings. His character serves
as "sharp reminders" of what she might be. Since, according to
Miller, she lacks the temperament to utter her desires and
follow them to their end, she must rely on Willy, through a
process of identification, for their expression. Of course, she
has developed an iron repression of her exceptions to his
weaknesses, for to recognize them would be to admit that her
deepest longings can never reach fulfillment.[4]

Over the past years authors of a growing body of feminist literature have analyzed the position of women in modern society. It has become increasingly clear how pervasively women have been encouraged not to seek fulfillment through their own accomplishments but through a passive identification with the accomplishments of their husbands (or other men). Although most women have accepted this dynamic as perfectly natural and even de-- sirable, there is evidence to show that these same women, although not consciously aware of it, are in fact terribly angry at their husbands. They must accept a secondary position; but having accepted that position, they are not fulfilled by their husbands' accomplishments. Behind the show of the "perfect wife" is often a woman bent on revenge. This desire can be so intense that the "perfect wife," while hiding these actions from herself and others, may actually be attempting to destroy her husband (or other men around her).

Linda, as we have seen, certainly falls into the general category of the "perfect wife." She appears to love Willy, tries to help and protect him, and attempts to act as a force to keep the family together. It is my contention, however, that beneath this surface show is a furious woman. She is furious at having to accept a secondary position and having to hope for her own fulfillment through an identification with Willy. And she is furious that his accomplishments in life are so meager. Unconsciously she works to exact revenge upon her husband and sons. She has learned to accomplish this end, as many women have, by demanding that the men relate to her as little boys relate to a demanding mother. In order to gain her love, they must accept their dependence on her, and any anger they harbor toward her must be directed at themselves. These conditions not met, she will engage in a series of tactics designed to force them back into the role of dependent little boys: Linda will not listen or respond to their emotional needs; Linda will substitute physical solutions for emotional needs; Linda will attack them for their weak qualities and blame them for their own feelings; Linda will take the side of whoever or whatever is annoying them; and Linda will never allow them more than a few moments of love and affection before attacking them again.

Far from acting as a healing agent, Linda is a central participant in the tragic action of the play.

7

At the beginning of <u>Death of a Salesman</u> something has
happened to Willy that is a significant landmark in the process
of his emotional disintegration. For the first time in his
selling life he has not been able to get past the first stage
of a trip. He finds himself incapable of keeping his mind on
his driving, and several times, at excessive speeds, almost goes
off the road. He is so frightened he comes home from Yonkers
at ten miles an hour. Linda, who has been asleep, wakes up
upon hearing him:

> Linda, <u>hearing Willy outside the bedroom,</u>
> <u>calls with some trepidation</u>: Willy!
>
> Willy: It's all right. I came back.
>
> Linda: Why? What happened? <u>Slight pause</u>.
> Did something happen, Willy?
>
> Willy: No, nothing happened.
>
> Linda: You didn't smash the car, did you?
>
> Willy, <u>with casual irritation</u>: I said
> nothing happened. Didn't you hear me?
>
> Linda: Don't you feel well?

Several aspects of this exchange should interest us.
Perhaps it is because his arrival is so unexpected, and perhaps
it is because Linda is frightened, but she shows little de-
light at Willy's returning home. Her welcome is rather negative. She stresses possibilities of deficiencies in his
character: something may have "happened," he may have smashed
the car, he may be sick. That such a welcome displeases Willy
can be seen in his immediate defensiveness. He denies that
anything "happened":

> No, nothing happened.
>
> . . . .
>
> I said nothing happened. Didn't you hear me?

He is also a bit angry: Miller notes he says the latter line
with "<u>casual irritation</u>." But, of course, something has
"happened," something terribly important and frightening. And
Willy must have a strong need to tell Linda, to try to communi-

cate to her what happened, for he immediately contradicts himself and begins to tell her about the trip, about the something that "happened":

> I got as far as a little above Yonkers. I stopped for a cup of coffee. Maybe it was the coffee. . . . I suddenly couldn't drive any more. The car kept going off onto the shoulder, y'know?

That Willy should allow Linda to hear such things about himself is unusual, for Willy is the kind of person who almost always hides his own weaknesses from himself and others. Indeed, he is here suggesting—in a tentative way to be sure—that there is something emotionally wrong with him. But rather than affirm that she has heard his message (that there may be something wrong with his mind), Linda signals that she has not listened. She ascribes the difficulty to a circumstantial cause:

> Oh. Maybe it was the steering again. I don't think Angelo knows the Studebaker.

This is not what Willy has been trying to say. He presses the point again that it is not something else, it is himself:

> No, it's me. Suddenly I realize I'm going sixty miles an hour and I don't remember the last five minutes. I'm—I can't seem to—keep my mind to it.

Here he is even more explicit. In saying he cannot "keep my mind to it" he is closer to trying to reveal that his problem is emotional. But she won't listen. Again she places the blame on something physical:

> Maybe it's your glasses. You never went for your new glasses.

Again, Willy tries to tell her it is himself: "No, I see everything." And he strongly hints again at some sort of emotional imbalance by stressing the extremely slow speed at which he drove home:

> I came back at ten miles an hour. It took me nearly four hours from Yonkers.

Once more Linda signals she has not heard the substance of his message. The difficulty is physical. He is overworked:

> Well, you'll just have to take a rest, Willy, you can't continue this way.

9

But Willy will not accept this evasion: "I just got back from Florida." Finally Linda agrees that the problem is in his mind, but she does it in such a way as to not agree. He is not emotionally imbalanced; his mind is "overactive", implying, again, some sort of physical malady.

Having been unable to communicate to the person closest in his life the terrors facing him, Willy now attempts to deal with these terrors by becoming less honest with himself, by trying to pass them off as an illusion. He pretends that he may be all right in the morning (a suggestion which contradicts everything he has been trying to tell Linda), and, following his wife's lead, projects his emotional pain on to something physical (the arch supports):

> I'll start out in the morning. Maybe I'll
> feel better in the morning. These goddam
> arch supports are killing me.

One would think that Linda would be disturbed by Willy's falling back on the use of rationalization—and the attendant loss of ability to find and solve the problem. Instead, she is ready with another solution that implies there is something physically wrong with him:

> Take an aspirin. Should I get you an
> aspirin? It'll sooth you.

But Willy's need to tell her what is really happening is very strong, and he makes another attempt:

> I was driving along, you understand? and I
> was fine. I was even observing the scenery.
> You can imagine, me looking at scenery, on
> the road every week of my life. But it's so
> beautiful up there, Linda, the trees are so
> thick, and the sun is warm. I opened the
> windshield and just let the warm air bathe
> over me. And then all of a sudden I'm goin'
> off the road! I'm tellin' ya, I absolutely
> forgot I was driving. . . . I have such
> thoughts, I have such strange thoughts.

Again, considering the way Willy usually hides what is going on inside of him, these lines are unique. They are the closest he will come in the play to describing to another person his inner terrors. The last lines, about having "such strange thoughts," are particularly important. Linda again signals she has not heard the substance of his message by once more offering a physical cause for his difficulties. He is too old. That is the basis of his problem:

> But you're sixty years old. They can't ex-
> pect you to keep traveling every week.

Again, Willy begins to pretend. He suggests that if only he
were able to see Brown and Morrison and show them the line,
"Goddamit, I could sell them." Furthermore,

> If old man Wagner were alive I'd a been in
> charge of New York now.

Linda encourages this lack of honesty: "Why don't you tell
those things to Howard, dear?" And when Willy seems heartened
by Linda, she has another physical solution ready: "I'll make
you a sandwich."

Willy's thoughts nevertheless quickly turn gloomy again,
and they center on Biff. It is clear that Willy idealizes Biff
and has invested heavily in the hope that Biff would be a great
success in life. The breach between Willy and Biff has, to say
the least, troubled Willy. Linda certainly understands the
outward dynamics of this situation. When Willy complains to
Linda:

> Figure it out. Work a lifetime to pay off
> a house. You finally own it, and there's
> nobody to live in it;

and when he asks, "Did Biff say anything after I went this
morning?"; Linda might say much to ease Willy's mind. She
might tell him she understands why Willy felt compelled to
start last night's argument with Biff (stupid as that argument
was) and she might try to show that in spite of all appearances
Biff does love Willy. And working from that base—a base of
understanding Willy's feelings—she might suggest ways for the
two to be reconciled. Instead, she <u>attacks</u> Willy:

> You shouldn't have criticized him, Willy,
> especially after he just got off the train.
> You mustn't lose your temper with him.

Such a remark is hardly helpful, for it not only causes Willy
to grow angry at her—the very person he needs understanding
from—but it causes him again to start lying to himself. He
claims that he did not lose his temper and that pointing out
Biff's failures did not constitute criticism:

> When the hell did I lose my temper? I
> simply asked him if he were making any
> money. Is that criticism?

Now, again, an intelligent course would be for Linda to indicate that she understands why he feels compelled to attack Biff. But she denies him this. Although later she, herself, will attack Biff for what he has done with his life, she now, in front of Willy, defends Biff:

> But, dear, how could he make any money?

Well, obviously, Biff could make money by working. But she has an excuse: "He's finding himself, Willy." Beyond the fact that she doesn't believe this (as we know from her attack on Biff later in the act), such a defense of their son has the immediate effect of causing Willy to attack him:

> Not finding yourself at the age of thirty-four is a disgrace.
>
> . . . .
>
> The trouble is he's lazy, goddammit!
>
> . . . .
>
> Biff is a lazy bum!
>
> . . . .
>
> Why did he come home? I would like to know what brought him home.

Yet Linda continues to defend Biff:

> I don't know. I think he's still lost, Willy. I think he's very lost.

At this point in the script we appear to be faced with a contradiction. Willy, as we have seen, has just been attacking Biff, calling him a lazy bum, and suddenly, for no apparent reason, he begins to defend Biff:

> Biff Loman is lost. In the greatest country in the world a young man with such--personal attractiveness, gets lost. And such a hard worker. There's one thing about Biff--he's not lazy.

In fact, Willy claims he will get Biff a job selling and that "He could be big in no time." How are we to explain Willy's sudden reversal? If we understand that Linda's constant refusal to listen to Willy's inner feelings has angered Willy and caused him to contradict her more and more and oppose her more and more, then we can see that she has now pushed him to argue

with her openly. It does not matter really what the subject is
or what side she takes. She has been arguing Biff is lost,
has she? He will argue that he is not lost. When to avoid his
anger she quickly changes the subject to the cheese she has
got him, he attacks that action:

> Why do you get American when I like Swiss?

When she tries to defend herself by saying she thought he would
like a change, he attacks that:

> I don't want a change! I want Swiss cheese.

And he states what he sees to be the truth of the situation:
"Why am I always being contradicted?" He lashes out directly
at her:

> Why don't you open a window in here, for
> God's sake?

When she blocks this attack by pointing out that the windows
are already open, rather than direct his anger to where it
belongs, he projects it onto the city which seems to be enclosing him:

> The street is lined with cars. There's not
> a breath of fresh air in the neighborhood.
> The grass don't grow anymore, you can't
> raise a carrot in the back yard. They
> should've had a law against apartment houses.

Linda continues to contradict Willy. She claims that "people
had to move somewhere." He disagrees: "No, there's more
people now." She contradicts him: "I don't think there's
more people. I think--" He fights back, and in attacking
the city is really attacking Linda who is "out of control" and
is "maddening":

> There's more people! That's what's ruining
> this country! Population is getting out of
> control. The competition is maddening!
> Smell the stink from the apartment house!
> And another on the other side. . . .

The type of new cheese she got him may have been accidental, but
Willy, after carrying on about the strangulating effects of over-
population, can suddenly, and seemingly out of nowhere, ask,
"How can they whip cheese?"[*]

---

[*]Unless otherwise indicated, all italics in quotes from
the play (other than stage directions) are mine.

That all this anger has been directed at Linda can be seen
in a sudden, and otherwise inexplicable change in Willy's
behavior. Miller notes that abruptly Willy turns "to Linda
guiltily." And suddenly he is solicitous of her:

> You're not worried about me, are you sweet-
> heart?
>
> . . . .
>
> You're my foundation and support, Linda.

Several conclusions can be reached from this sudden change of
behavior. First, Willy feels guilty toward Linda. He feels
guilty, in my opinion, because she has managed to enrage him
and he has been engaged in a violent attack on her. Now his
feelings of guilt about attacking her have overwhelmed him.
Second, he wants to make sure that his attack has not caused
him to lose her. He indicates to her that he is really dependent
upon her, that he is the one who relies upon her. She is his
"foundation and support." He will not argue with her anymore.
Third, and most interestingly, now that Willy has adopted this
new attitude, Linda for the first time in the play supports him
and calms him:

> You've got too much on the ball to worry
> about.
>
> . . . .
>
> Just try to relax, dear.

In quick summary, then, Linda has managed to get Willy to
relate to her as a small, dependent boy. She has done this by
not allowing him to communicate his deep needs to her, attempting
to find physical solutions for these needs, stressing his weak
qualities, taking Biff's side against him, and blaming him for
his own feelings. She offers him his reward, love and support,
only when he becomes dependent upon her.

But this reward does not last long.

Almost immediately Linda attacks Willy with such force
that he retreats into a hallucination in order to escape from
her:

> Linda: And Willy--if it's warm Sunday we'll
> drive in the country. And we'll open the
> windshield, and take lunch.
>
> Willy: No, the windshields don't open on the

new cars.

Linda: But you opened it today.

Willy: Me. I didn't. He stops. Now isn't
that peculiar! Isn't that a remarkable--He
breaks off in amazement and fright as the flute
is heard distantly.

Linda: What, darling?

Willy: That is the most remarkable thing.

Linda: What, dear?

Willy: I was thinking of the Chevy. Slight
pause. Nineteen twenty-eight. . .when I had
that red Chevy--Breaks off. That funny? I
coulda sworn I was driving that Chevy today.

Linda: Well, that's nothing. Something
must've reminded you.

At the beginning of these lines Willy is relaxed and fairly
happy, and at the end of it he is hallucinating. Evidently
what has caused this sudden change is his discovery that he
was in fact hallucinating earlier in the day when he believed
himself to be driving the old Chevy with the windshield open.
It is Linda who mentions the windshield ("And we'll open the
windshield. . ."). When Willy corrects her and explains that
windshields don't open on the new cars, Linda insists, "But
you opened it today." Here we must make a decision. Is Linda
unaware that windshields on new cars don't open? Windshields
that could be opened on family cars were discontinued in the
early thirties. It hardly seems possible that in the late
forties Linda thinks windshields open; moreover, she must have
ridden in the new Studebaker. So, if she knows windshields
don't open in new cars, why does she suggest to Willy that
they open it when they go on the picnic? And even if one wanted
to argue that she brings the subject up as an honest mistake,
why, after Willy has pointed out that the windshields on new
cars don't open, does she insist, "But you opened it today"?
The answer must be that consciously or unconsciously she wants
to remind Willy of his emotional problems. Thus when Willy
says he "coulda sworn I was driving that Chevy today," Linda
denies any responsibility of bringing it to his attention:
"Well, that's nothing. Something must've reminded you."

We can understand Willy's turning to the refuge of hallucination at the end of this scene as an escape from a long series
of disagreeable ploys by Linda, the windshield incident standing

15

as the last in the series. Because Willy cannot stand up to the strength of her attack, he gives up. Although Linda would never consciously admit the possibility, she seems to want to pull the emotional supports out from under her "child" until he becomes psychologically disabled.

III

A brief argument between Biff and Willy precedes the next scene that is exclusively between Linda and Willy. Happy has suggested his Florida water polo idea, Biff has agreed that it might work, and Willy has reacted ecstatically. Unfortunately, a bitter argument develops between Biff and his father, and Willy, suddenly crestfallen and angered, leaves for bed. Linda also seems crestfallen. She asks Biff,

> What'd you have to start that for? You see how sweet he was as soon as you talked hope-fully?

And she makes what appears to be a good suggestion:

> Come up and say good night to him. Don't let him go to bed that way.

When Biff offers some resistance, she asks again:

> Please, dear. Just say good night. It takes so little to make him happy. Come.

In fact, her suggestion is a very good one. When Biff does come up and says a pleasant good night to Willy, Willy is pleased and appears to forget the bitter argument of several minutes ago.

Linda's own actions toward Willy, however, are more open to question. She precedes the boys to the bedroom, and her entrance finds Willy in the bathroom. Presumably she will follow her own advice to Biff and say something pleasant and reassuring. Instead she says:

> Can you do something about the shower? It drips.

One of the constant irritants in Willy's life is the breakdown of mechanical things. Various failings of the house, the car, and the refrigerator anger him greatly. Her remark, then, is

16

hardly calculated to make him feel better. In fact, it starts
him off in the wrong direction:

> All of a sudden everything falls to pieces.
> Goddam plumbing, oughta be sued, those
> people. I hardly finished putting in the
> thing. . . .

Having made this initial mistake, Linda might now reverse herself and find something to say to build up Willy's sense of
assurance. Again, she does the opposite:

> I'm just wondering if Oliver will remember
> him [Biff]. You think he might?

We must remember that only minutes before Willy was ecstatically
contemplating the future success of the water polo team which
depended for its financial backing on Oliver. Even Linda
thought it was all a good idea. Now she suggests that Oliver
may not be counted on. And, as we would suspect, Willy is
defensive:

> Remember him? What's the matter with you,
> you crazy? If he'd've stayed with Oliver
> he'd be on top now! Wait'll Oliver gets a
> look at him.

At this point the boys come in, and the conversation between
Biff and Willy goes reasonably well. Willy, after Biff leaves,
becomes contented and relaxed and indulges in some fond memories
of Biff:

> Like a young god. Hercules—something like
> that. And the sun, the sun all around him.
> Remember how he waved to me? Right up from
> the field, with the representatives of three
> colleges standing by?

Linda should be content. If anything, she might encourage him
along the thought pattern he is following. It is almost in-
credible, then, that she asks: "Willy dear, what has he got
against you?" This attack disturbs Willy, for, although up to
this point he has shown no signs of wishing to go to sleep and
has been quite talkative, now he can say, "I'm so tired. Don't
talk any more."

The end of the scene resembles a tableau of mother and
child. Linda has picked away at the props supporting his self-
respect, and when Willy gets into bed she asks, "Should I sing
to you?" Of all the types of songs she might choose, "_Linda_
hums _a_ _soft_ lullaby." Willy's final line is that of a boy. He

has warned Biff not to say "Gee" since "Gee" is a boy's word.
But the act closes with Willy saying,

> Gee, look at the moon moving between the
> buildings.

This to "Linda's desperate but monotonous humming. . . ."

IV

An unusual aspect of the first scene in the second act is
that it is the only extended period in the play where Willy is
at all relaxed and contented. He appears confident that Biff
will be successful with Oliver, that he, himself, will be able
to work in New York; perhaps most important of all, he has
gotten a good night's sleep. And in this sense the scene is a
good one for us to study, for if there is a time in the play
when Linda should most easily be able to help keep Willy happy,
this is it. Yet something goes wrong. Although the scene is
relatively short (covering about five pages in my edition) Willy
loses his temper twice and leaves the house in a bad mood.

In order to analyze the scene it is important to determine
whether Linda actually thinks Biff will be successful in his
negotiations with Oliver. If she does, then much of what she
says later in the scene doesn't appear to make sense. When
Willy asks her how much Biff will ask Oliver for, she replies,
"He didn't mention it, but I imagine ten or fifteen thousand."
Now, clearly this is big money (keeping in mind this is the late
forties). The amount contrasts sharply with the two hundred
dollars Linda tells Willy they need to tide them over until
the next month. It is inconceivable that if Biff were actually
able to get that kind of money, he couldn't spare enough to
help his parents through their immediate financial difficulties.
Therefore, if Linda believes Biff will be successful in getting
this kind of money, why does she bring up to Willy a number of
outstanding bills?

> Linda: And Willy, don't forget to ask for a
> little advance, because we've got the in-
> surance premium. It's the grace period now.
>
> Willy: That's a hundred. . .?
>
> Linda: A hundred and eight, sixty-eight.
> Because we're a little short again.

> Willy: Why are we short?
>
> Linda: Well, you had the motor job on the car. . . .
>
> Willy: That goddam Studebaker!
>
> Linda: And you got one more payment on the refrigerator. . .
>
> Willy: But it just broke again.

The other alternative is not attractive either. Let us suppose Linda does not believe Biff will be successful with Oliver (and there seem to be a number of clues to support this in the play). Then why does she pretend she does, since her building up of Biff puts Willy in a bad light in comparison? Biff, according to Linda, looked

> so handsome in that suit. He could be a—— anything in that suit.

But when Willy suggests that he, himself, can accomplish something, too, by planting some seeds in the back yard, Linda is cold to the idea:

> But not enough sun gets back there. Nothing'll grow any more.

And she couples the enormous amount of money Biff is going to ask for with her reminder that Willy must, in effect, beg for the favor of being given a slot in the home office:

> He [Biff] didn't mention it, but I imagine ten or fifteen thousand. You going to talk to Howard today?

Whether or not Linda believes Biff will be able to get money from Oliver, she manages to make Willy angry. But rather than direct his anger at Linda he projects it on the failings of the mechanical things around him:

> Whoever heard of a Hastings refrigerator. Once in my life I would like to own something outright before it's broken! I'm always in a race with the junkyard!

One more payment on the house, as Linda points out, will be the last, and in an attempt to rebuild his injured self-esteem, Willy magnifies the importance of this fact. He calls it a "great thing." Linda, however, only says, "It's an accomplishment." Willy points out all the

cement, the lumber, the reconstruction I put
in this house! There ain't a crack to be
found in it any more.

Linda appears unimpressed. "Well, it's served its purpose."
Willy is hurt by her remark:

What purpose? Some stranger'll come along,
move in, and that's that.

Having thus demeaned his accomplishments, Linda remembers
to remind Willy that the boys are going to treat him to a big
celebrative dinner that night, and for the second time in the
scene Willy is enthusiastic and happy:

Gee, whiz. That's really somethin'. I'm
gonna knock Howard for a loop, kid. I'll
get an advance, and I'll come home with a
New York job. Goddammit, now I'm gonna do
it.

Yet a glance at the end of the scene will show that Willy leaves
the house dejected and angry:

Linda: It's changing, Willy. I can feel it
changing!

Willy: Beyond a question. G'by, I'm late.
He starts to go again.

Linda, calling after him as she runs to the
kitchen table for a handkerchief: You got
your glasses?

Willy, feels for them, then comes back in:
Yeah, yeah, got my glasses.

Linda, giving him the handkerchief: And a
handkerchief.

Willy: Yeah, handkerchief.

Linda: And your saccharine?

Willy: Yeah, my saccarine.

Linda: Be careful on the subway stairs.

She kisses him, and a silk stocking is seen
hanging from her hand. Willy notices it.

20

Willy: Will you stop mending stockings?
At least while I'm in the house. It gets
me nervous. I can't tell you. Please.

Although Willy is upset about the stockings which symbolize for
him his guilty affair with the woman in Boston, his nervousness
is more likely caused by Linda's mothering. She treats him
not as a man but as a small boy. He has just told her he is
going to really act like a "man": he's going to knock Howard
for a loop, get an advance, and "do it." But his enthusiasm
melts as she asks whether he has his glasses, his handkerchief,
his saccharine, and cautions him to be careful on the subway
stairs. Demeaned, he explodes at her; and the silk stockings,
like the refrigerator and the car earlier in the scene, provides a convenient excuse. Again, as he leaves the house, he
tries once more to convince himself he can accomplish something: "Maybe beets would grow out there." But she denies
him even this gesture: "But you tried so many times."

Once more, then, we see Linda using the ploys of the controlling mother: she builds up another man (Biff), reminds
Willy of his weaknesses, demeans his accomplishments, worries
about his petty physical needs, and doesn't allow him more than
a moment of contentment.

V

The play contains another kind of evidence that Linda acts
as a controlling mother. So far we have been inspecting her
interchanges with Willy which occur, as it were, in reality.
Miller allows us access to a number of Willy's hallucinations.
Although we cannot trust any of these hallucinations to mirror
events as they actually happened in the past, they provide us
with important clues about how Willy _feels_ about members of his
family and how he perceives their actions toward him. Willy's
hallucinations can best be understood as invented material,
and can be analyzed as dreams are analyzed.

Willy's first hallucination occurs after Linda "reminded"
him that he opened the windshield of his car. In this hallucination he falls back on his favorite line of defense against
Linda's ploys: a good relationship with his boys—especially
Biff. In Willy's mind the boys apply loving care to the
symbol of his success, the Chevy; they tell him they were lone-
some for him, and they are in awe of his great business deals.
In particular Willy hallucinates about the upcoming big football
game, for it symbolizes all his hope that Biff will become the

21

embodiment of the American dream. That this hallucination starts out as an escape from Linda can also be seen in this unrealistic detail: Willy has just returned from a trip, yet has not greeted Linda but is spending his time with the boys. When Willy does have Linda appear, however, things begin to go wrong. Linda suggests that Biff go down to the cellar to take care of his numerous friends there, but Biff, in effect, disobeys her. "Ah, when Pop comes home they can wait!" But when Willy suggests Biff go down, he goes, saying that he'll have them sweep out the furnace room. Rather than pointing out that Biff has obeyed Willy—a remark which would buoy Willy's confidence—Linda points out that the boys obey <u>Biff</u>. Willy attempts to bring the subject back to himself. "Well, that's the training, the training." That is, Biff is able to order others around because of Willy's training. And Willy tries in another way to build himself up. "I'm tellin' you, I was sellin' thousands and thousands, but I had to come home." Linda acts as if she has not heard him: "Oh, the whole block'll be at that game." The remark is a non-sequitur, but it does have the effect, again, of building up Biff. And even though Willy has just said he was selling thousands and thousands, she can ask, "Did you sell anything?"

In the same hallucination, Willy has Linda probe until she unmasks the fact he hasn't done very well at all on the trip. Willy first claims that he did five hundred gross in Providence and seven hundred gross in Boston, but when she presses him ("How much did you do?") he drops the figure to "roughly" two hundred gross for the "whole" trip. Naturally, Willy is angered and begins to project his failings on some stores in Boston:

> The trouble was that three of the stores were half closed for inventory in Boston. Other-
> wise I woulda broke records.

His anger increases as Linda points out the bills he owes on the refrigerator, the washing machine, the vacuum cleaner, the roof and the car. Willy's anger at her takes the form of attacking these mechanical objects. What is noteworthy, however, is that rather than sympathize with Willy, Linda <u>takes the side of the companies that made the machines</u>. For example, Willy owes sixteen dollars on the refrigerator:

> Willy: Why sixteen?
>
> Linda: Well, the fan belt broke, so it was a dollar eighty.
>
> Willy: But it's brand new.

> Linda: Well, the man said that's the way
> it is. Till they work themselves in, y'know.

Willy obviously has a good point. If the refrigerator is new,
it shouldn't be breaking belts. At least as far as fan belts
go, the refrigerator seems to be a lemon; the repairman has
handed Linda a rationalization designed to protect his organiza-
tion. But Linda, by passing along the rationalization, is, in
effect, taking the side of the company against Willy. When
Willy worries, "I hope we didn't get stuck on that machine,"
again Linda takes the side of the company: "They got the
biggest ads of any of them." Willy's reply is defensive and
angry: "I know, it's a fine machine."

Next, we see another example of Linda's refusal to listen
to Willy's expression of his honest emotional needs. He begins
to confess to a number of weaknesses which apparently really
bother him:

> You know, the trouble is Linda, people don't
> seem to take to me.

As in his real life, Linda doesn't listen to this honest expression of an emotional need: "Oh, don't be foolish." But
he insists:

> I know it when I walk in. They seem to laugh
> at me.

Again she refuses to hear him:

> Why would they laugh at you? Don't talk that
> way, Willy.

He repeats that people just pass him by, that he's not noticed.
She denies it, says he's doing wonderfully. He says he talks
too much. She replies that he's only "lively." He says that
he's fat, that "I'm very--foolish to look at, Linda," that
someone said he was like a walrus. But she insists that he's
the most handsome man in the world.

Now, at this point in the hallucination we hear a woman's
rather mocking laughter. Manifestly, it is the woman in
Boston, the woman Willy had an affair with. There is no logical
reason why Willy should bring her in at this time. Nothing in
the surface content of the hallucination has reminded him of
her. But, of course, since the hallucination can be treated
as a dream nothing has to be logical--at least on the surface.
On one level the woman in Boston is a form of Linda. That is,
on the manifest level Linda may be supporting Willy, but in
fact she has Willy so confused, that her praising him (which,

23

as we have seen is here a way of not listening to him) is a
final thrust of mockery. And the woman's laughter, which is to
say Linda's laughter, is Willy's perception of what Linda really
thinks of him. How does Willy react to this perception? He
becomes even more dependent on Linda!

> with great feeling: You're the best there is,
> Linda, you're a pal, you know that?

But the stage directions indicate that the woman's laughter "is
loud now." Linda's laughter and the woman's are blended
together at one point: "The Woman bursts out laughing, and
Linda's laughter blends in." At this point Linda is telling
Willy, "You are, Willy, the handsomest man." We are not
surprised, therefore, to find Willy exploding in anger at Linda,
although he projects that anger on to the stockings:

> angrily, taking them from her: I won't have
> you mending stockings in this house! Now
> throw them out!

Mending stockings, of course, is a mother's chore, and Willy
attacks Linda's motherly role.

Besides the attack over the stockings, Willy demonstrates
his anger toward her in other ways. In expressing his
dependency upon her, there is also the hint that he wishes to
kill her:

> On the road--on the road I want to grab you
> sometimes and just kiss the life outa you.

And he has the Woman in Boston--and this woman is, as we have
seen, at least a form of Linda--say,

> You just kill me, Willy. He suddenly grabs
> her and kisses her roughly. You kill me.

In any case, the defense Willy was originally using in the
hallucination to protect himself against Linda disintegrates.
In the first part of the hallucination, Biff and Happy, but
particularly Biff, admire him for his manly deeds. Biff is
going to be successful in life. But after Willy's talk with
Linda, that dream falls apart. Biff is in trouble. Bernard
runs in and says, "Where is he? If he doesn't study!" Linda
cautions,

> And he'd better give back that football,
> Willy, it's not nice.

Willy wonders why "is he taking everything?" and exclaims, "I'll

24

whip him." Bernard adds that "He's driving the car without a license!" In the midst of this, "The Woman's laugh is heard." Willy tries to stop the laugh: "Shut up!" Linda explains, "All the mothers--", and Willy says the same thing to her he said to the Woman's laughter: "Shut up!" Bernard warns that "If he doesn't buckle down he'll flunk math." Linda agrees: "He's right, Willy, you gotta--". And the hallucination ends with Willy's anger at Linda at full force:

> exploding at her: There's nothing the matter with him!

In this hallucination Linda repeats the patterns we have already noticed in her--not listening to Willy's need to communicate his emotional pain, building up other people, mentioning things that annoy Willy, and pointing out his weaknesses. Moreover, if we look at the hallucination in its full sweep, and if we remember to treat it as a dream, we see that Linda spoils Willy's attempt at seeing himself as a worthwhile person. He gets along fine with his sons until she comes in and ruins everything. Since this dream is not real, it does not constitute direct evidence that Linda acts towards him as a controlling mother, but since it does not contradict evidence drawn from the real events in the play, we have reason to believe that Willy's image of Linda in this hallucination is realistic.

VI

Clearly Linda knows as well as anyone that Willy is losing his grip on reality. She knows he is suicidal. The insurance man has explained to her that Willy's car accidents were probably not accidents, and she has discovered a device in the basement which Willy apparently has considered using to kill himself. In other words, it must be clear to her that Willy is suffering from extreme emotional difficulties and that his life is in danger. But oddly enough, when Linda is talking to her sons, she initially denies that his problems are emotional:

> Linda: You called him crazy--
>
> Biff: I didn't mean--
>
> Linda: No, a lot of people think he's lost his--balance. But you don't have to be very smart to know what his trouble is. The man is exhausted.

25

Not only does Linda here deny what is obvious, that Willy has lost his balance, but she makes another interesting slip. She charges Biff with having called Willy "crazy." But Biff has not called Willy crazy. Happy brought the word up, and did it in such a way as to deny it:

> Happy: He's always had respect for—
>
> Biff: What the hell do you know about it?
>
> Happy, surlily: Just don't call him crazy!

That is, even though Biff has not called Willy crazy, Linda is sensitive enough on the subject to project that he has. But, according to her, his charge—even though he hasn't made it—is wrong. Willy is only "exhausted":

> A small man can be just as exhausted as a great man.

And what is the cause of his "exhaustion"? It is, first of all, the company's fault:

> He works for a company thirty-six years this March, opens up unheard-of territories to their trademark, and now in his old age they take his salary away.

Secondly, the old buyers have died:

> But now his old friends, the old buyers that loved him so and always found some order to hand him in a pinch—they're all dead, retired.

Thirdly, his sons have turned on him:

> The man who never worked a day but for your benefit? When does he get a medal for that?

More specifically, it is Biff's fault: "It's when you come home he's always the worst." Now, of course, all these factors have contributed to Willy's emotional difficulties. What is interesting, however, is that Linda makes herself out to be blameless. Not that it has been easy for her:

> I don't know what to do. I live from day to day, boys. I tell you, I know every thought in his mind.

Unlike the others, she loves him:

26

He's the dearest man in the world to me, and
I won't have anyone making him feel unwanted
and low and blue.

Again, unlike the others, she pays him the attention he
deserves:

But he's a human being, and a terrible thing
is happening to him. So attention must be
paid. He's not to be allowed to fall into
his grave like an old dog.

The picture she paints is of a man, loved and protected by her,
who is not coming apart emotionally, but rather is "exhausted"
due to the mistreatment of others. And when she is forced to
admit that Willy is disturbed, she denies any ugly thoughts
toward him:

With great difficulty: Oh, boys, it's so
hard to say a thing like this! He's just
a big stupid man to you, but I tell you
there's more good in him than in many other
people.

Her defensiveness toward her own feelings about Willy
comes out most clearly in the Requiem. We would expect to find
Linda torn apart by grief at his funeral. On the contrary,
Linda remains strangely unmoved:

Linda doesn't react. She stares at the
grave. . . . Linda makes no move.

And, as she says, "I can't cry." Strangely, she wonders why
Willy killed himself. Before, as we have just seen, she had
all sorts of explanations, but now "I can't understand it."
She offers one clue: he killed himself due to his financial
worries:

First time in thirty-five years we were
just about free and clear. He only needed
a little salary. He was even finished with
the dentist.

Charlie points out the obvious by suggesting that there must
have been much more involved than financial worries ("No man
only needs a little salary."), but when she is left alone with
him she still attempts to connect his suicide to money worries:

I don't understand it. Why did you ever do
that? . . . Why did you do it? I search and
search and I search, and I can't understand

27

it, Willy. I made the last payment on the
house today.

For all her searching she cannot understand, and has come up
with only one rather weak explanation. Nor can she cry. This
inability ("Forgive me dear, I can't cry. . .") might be explained by what Miller, in his opening description of her, has
called her "iron repression." But, in fact, she is quite
capable of crying. For example, talking to Biff in the first
act she is at one point

> bent over the chair, weeping, her face in
> her hands.

I suggest that her inability to cry, her refusal to admit
that Willy is emotionally disturbed, and her attempts to place
the blame elsewhere can be seen as extreme defensiveness. Her
own guilt is too close to the surface. Willy's breakdown and
death must be inexplicable. His suicide cannot in any way be
connected with her desires. And when she does break, her
crying is not related to grief but to release and joy:

> We're free and clear. Sobbing more fully,
> released: We're free.

These are her final words, and one cannot escape the juxtaposition of Willy's death, her lack of grief, her words about
freedom, and her emotional release at the mention of freedom.
She must disguise her joy that she, not a man, has been
victorious.

VII

Another juxtaposition at the end of the Requiem should
not escape our attention. As Linda breaks emotionally and
cries out, "We're free. . . . We're free. . . . We're
free. . .," "Biff comes slowly toward her" and "lifts her to
her feet and moves out right with her in his arms." Since
earlier in the same speech she refers to Willy as "you" ("Why
did you ever do that?"), it is possible to wonder if the "we"
she repeats in this very last phrase may not mean Biff rather
than Willy. As she sobs "more fully, released," are certain
feelings toward Biff coming unguarded to the surface? Does
Willy's death no longer stand in the way of a longing for Biff
she has secretly had--a relationship which is symbolized by
Biff taking her away with "her in his arms"?

Such a notion is certainly theoretically more than possible. Typically a woman who, due to her own need to dominate her husband turns him into a dependent little boy therefore incapable of being a "man" to her, hopes to find fulfillment for her emotional needs in her son. But her longing toward her son has a double edge. On the one hand, she secretly hopes that, unlike her childish husband, the son will be masterful enough to resist her hostility and successfully overwhelm her. On the other hand, it is just such mastery against which she has so desperately fought. Her son, therefore, constitutes an even greater danger than her husband. Because of the intensity of this hope and fear, her attempts to keep the son a child are even more desperate than those directed at her husband. And given a choice between husband and son, since she desires and therefore fears the son more, she will choose the emasculated husband over the son.

In the long scene between Linda and Biff in the first act Linda's motivation appears to be to get Biff to act decently to Willy. This analysis is correct only to a point. However, Linda's primary interest here is not to help or protect Willy, but to act out her own needs in relation to Biff. That is, she works to reduce him to the level of a dependent child. She cannot allow him any form of independence. And if we skip, for the moment, to the end of this long scene, we can see that she has been successful toward that end. Biff kneels to Linda:

> kissing her: All right, pal, all right.
> It's all settled now. I've been remiss.
> I know that, Mom. But now I'll stay, and
> I swear to you, I'll apply myself.
> Kneeling in front of her, in a fever of
> self-reproach. . . .

Biff's reaction is somewhat similar to Willy's near the end of the first Willy-Linda scene where Willy acts both guilty and dependent on her. In the present scene, Biff's anger is turned against himself in "a fever of self-reproach." He kneels to Linda to show his submission to her; he kisses her to show his devotion; he agrees to live at home; and he vows to go into business, a way of life which for him means giving up a sense of his own individuality.

Linda makes Biff dependent by using somewhat the same ploys she uses on Willy: she does not listen to or respond to his needs; she attempts to make him feel guilty about his own feelings; and she takes the side of his competitor—Willy.

Linda's lack of response to Biff's needs is an aspect of her behavior that is easily overlooked. Biff has his troubles.

29

He is a confused adolescent at the age of 35. He has drifted
from job to job, has a history of stealing, has been in jail;
even when he is seemingly happy on a job, he panics and comes
running home. Although Linda appears very understanding of
Biff when she is with Willy, she has no patience for Biff's
difficulties when she is with him. Not once in the play does
she express any interest in or concern for his difficulties.
Even at the end of the second act Linda does not bother to ask
whether or not Biff was successful in getting the money from
Oliver.

When Biff comes downstairs after the bedroom scene with
Happy, his anger at Willy should be apparent to Linda:

> What is he doing out there?
>
> . . . .
>
> God almighty, Mom, how long has he been doing
> this?
>
> . . . .
>
> What the hell is the matter with him?

If Linda wanted to deal with this anger so as to reconcile Biff
and Willy, she would try to listen to Biff. She would attempt
to understand _why_ Biff is angry and to a degree sympathize with
him. Biff might then reveal his emotions so they could be discussed rationally; thus Biff would have a better chance to feel
at least some sort of dignity, which is necessary for reconcilia-
tion. But this dignity is not Linda's object. Therefore, she
does not listen and does not understand. When Biff accuses Willy
by asking what he's "doing out there?", Linda's response is:
"Sh!" When he tries to downgrade Willy, she replies, "Don't,
he'll hear you." And when he attempts to say that Willy is
acting improperly ("What the hell is the matter with him?"), she
disagrees: "It'll pass by morning." In all this, of course,
she implies that Biff is somehow to blame, and now she makes
that implication more explicit. Biff is in the wrong for not
having written letters. He should have written so that Willy
might "know that there's still the possibility for better things."
Not only has Biff failed here, but, illogically, he is still to
blame when he comes home--an action which should be far more
satisfactory than writing:

> It's when you come home he's always the worst.

Therefore, according to Linda, if Biff stays away he is at fault,
and if he comes home he is at fault. The problem with Biff,
Linda implies, is that he is angry with Willy. Biff evidently

understands the thrust of her argument because he now begins to
lie to Linda: "evasively: I'm not hateful, Mom."

There is good reason to believe that if Linda were really
concerned with Willy's welfare she would advise Biff never to
come home again since, according to her, they fight whenever
they are together. Linda, in fact, is able to take that position
at the end of the second act:

> I think that's the best way, dear [for Biff
> to leave and never come back]. 'Cause there's
> no use drawing it out, you'll just never get
> along.

(We will address ourselves later to the issue of why she takes
this position at the end of the play.) But her concern is to
confuse and weaken Biff, and so now, having accused Biff of
hurting Willy by coming home, she insists that Biff stay home:

> Are you home to stay now?
>
> . . . .
>
> Biff, you can't look around all your life,
> can you?
>
> . . . .
>
> Biff, a man is not a bird, to come and go with
> the springtime.

Biff attempts to escape from this double-bind by offering her
what he senses she wants: his love:

> Your hair. . . . He touches her hair. Your
> hair got so grey.

But she can accept his love only on her terms. He must not
show any independence, any mastery. He must efface himself.
Specifically, he must subjugate himself to the father he hates:

> Biff, dear, if you don't have any feeling for
> him, then you can't have any feeling for me.

Biff tries to disagree: "Sure I can, Mom." But she will not let
him off:

> No. You can't just come to see me, because
> I love him. With a threat, but only a threat
> of tears. He's the dearest man in the world
> to me, and I won't have anyone making him

feel unwanted and low and blue.

The bind is perfect. In order to give and get love from Linda, Biff must deny his hatred toward the man that Linda loves more than Biff ("He's the dearest man in the world to me. . ."). And if Biff doesn't do this, she threatens to cry, and he will be responsible for hurting her.

Biff reacts violently to this ploy:

> Stop making excuses for him. He always,
> always wiped the floor with you.

Furthermore, Willy has "no character." No one else would spew out "that vomit" from his mind. Linda responds in two ways. First, just as she defended Biff to Willy, now she defends Willy to Biff. Willy Loman may not have been a great man, he may not have made a lot of money or had his name in the paper,

> But he's a human being, and a terrible thing
> is happening to him. He's not to be allowed
> to fall into his grave like an old dog. At-
> tention, attention must finally be paid to
> such a person.

Second, she continues to blame Biff for Willy's troubles and thus to make Biff feel guilty for his own feelings. She charges that Biff called Willy "crazy" (something he did not do), and claims that Willy is upset because of his sons, particularly Biff. Willy "never worked a day but for your benefit," and now Biff has turned on him, when he and Willy used to be pals:

> How you used to talk to him on the phone
> every night! How lonely he was till he
> could come home to you.

Linda seems somewhat successful, for Biff tentatively agrees to curb his anger at his father:

> All right, Mom, I'll live here in my room,
> and I'll get a job. I'll keep away from
> him, that's all.

Linda's response to this offer doesn't appear to make sense:

> No, Biff. You can't stay here and fight all
> the time.

But Biff has just said he will stay away from Willy, and if he stays away from Willy, he can't fight him. What Biff means, of course, by "stay[ing] away from Willy" is that he will not be

friendly to him. And that is not enough for Linda. Biff seems
to realize in some way what she is asking of him, because having
made his offer, he turns on the stairs and says to Linda,

> furiously: I hate this city and I'll stay
> here. Now what do you want?

What she wants is Biff's total submission and dependence.

In order to get this submission she, in effect, accuses
Biff of murder. Willy has been trying to kill himself in a
variety of ways. And the responsibility for Willy's impending
death rests on Biff:

> I tell you he put his whole life into you and
> you've turned your backs on him.

She can claim, "I swear to God, Biff, his life is in your hands."
And now she carries out what was before a threat of crying:

> She is bent over in the chair, weeping, her
> face in her hands.

Through her crying her message is clear. She is asking Biff to
love her. But he can only stop her from crying if he blames
himself for his own feelings toward his father. And, as we have
seen, she is successful. Biff again promises to stay home and
get a job—the very thing he promised a number of lines before.
But now his tone is different. There is no independence, no
backbone. He is no longer outraged by what she wants. He now
shows his love to her while blaming himself: "kneeling in front
of her, in a fever of self-reproach. . . ."

VIII

If Linda has managed to get Biff to love her on her own
terms, why does she agree that Biff should leave at the end of
the play? Indeed, in this last confrontation she is desperate
that he do just that:

> Get out of my sight! Get out of here!

The answer is that her success in vanquishing Biff's independence
is only temporary. For reasons I will discuss in the next
chapter, Biff finally refuses to turn his feelings toward Willy
against himself. The incident in Oliver's office causes that
anger to break to the surface again, and he tries to confront

his father in the restaurant. Frustrated there, when he returns
home he is more than ever violently angry with Willy. His lines
make it clear that this time he will not be stopped.

> I wanna see the boss.

> . . . .

> Where is he? He moves toward the living room
> [looking for Willy] and Linda follows.

> . . . .

> I gotta talk to the boss, Mom. Where is he?

Linda makes a desperate effort to rein Biff in, to assert her
control over him.

> You're not going near him.

> . . . .

> I don't want you tormenting him any more.

> . . . .

> You're not going near him.

> . . . .

> You're not talking to him.

But she cannot control him, and it is she who is

> suddenly pleading: Will you please leave him
> alone?

Even her attempts to make him feel guilty for his anger do not
work now. When she says

> violently to Biff: Don't you care whether
> he lives or dies?,

Biff simply answers that "Nobody's dying around here, pal." She
shouts after Biff,

> You invite him for dinner. He looks forward
> to it all day. . . ,

but Biff simply ignores her and keeps looking for Willy. When
she calls her sons "animals" and accuses Biff of not "even

go[ing] in to see if he was all right!", Biff refuses to be
intimidated. Linda is unable to keep Biff away from Willy; when
Biff brings Willy back in he, Biff, is able to say that they
have "had it out." When Biff adds, "That clears it, doesn't it?"
and wants Willy to wish him luck, Linda is in favor of Biff
going. "Shake his hand, Willy." But, in fact, they have not
had it out. The real confrontation now takes place before Linda
(and later, Happy). Both Biff and Willy go for each other, and
Linda does what she can to stop Biff.

> Biff! _She moves to grab the hose, but Biff_
> _holds it down with his hand._

> . . . .

> Stop it!

> . . . .

> Don't, Biff.

But Biff has his confrontation with Willy. Exhausted, he
announces he will leave in the morning, and goes up the stairs
to his room. Biff has been successful in escaping from Linda--
at least for the time being--and now she has only two men, Happy
and Willy. And significantly, she calls them both "boys."
While Happy is turning to go up the stairs and Willy remains
in the room hallucinating, she can say,

> Be good. You're both good boys, just act
> that way, that's all.

Chapter II

BIFF

I

If previous writers on the play have ignored Linda's direct involvement in the tragic action, they have misjudged Biff's. An analysis of his deeper feelings is obscured by the ease with which it is possible to identify him as the tragic hero. It is conventional wisdom that a major character in a tragedy ought to learn something from the depth of his suffering. In this regard, as any number of critics have argued, Willy's actions are not tragic since he commits suicide paying allegiance to the ideals of the American system which misled him in life. Biff, on the other hand, seems to have understood something very important about himself in the course of the play: no less than who he is. Near the end of the second act Biff can tell his father, "Today I realized something about myself," and in the Requiem he can explain what that something is: "I know who I am." As Hagopian argues,

> it is Biff Loman who is seeking to "find himself"
> and does so in making an anguished choice between
> clear-cut alternatives--continued drifting or
> redeeming himself. . . . Biff is a man who
> ultimately makes things happen, who responds to
> the great trauma in his life first with an
> emotional and moral paralysis, and then with a
> determined effort to face the truth at whatever
> cost [1963, p. 118].

It has even been suggested that Biff's actions as a tragic hero justify Willy's suicide. Without that suicide, or at least without the events that led up to it and made it inevitable, Biff would never have found his inner knowledge. Parker claims:

> But even in Death of A Salesman there is one
> positive gain: Biff at least comes out of the
> experience with enhanced self-knowledge. . . .

It has been objected, and admitted by Miller, that Willy's stature as a tragic hero is questionable because he dies self-deceived. But the new truth is there in Biff, and the extension of expressionistic technique beyond Willy's death unbroken into the "Requiem" bends together the two experiences [1969, pp. 108, 109].

What is it that Biff comes to understand about himself? What is the nature of this new self-knowledge? The answer, of course, is complicated. Part of Biff's discovery is his realization that he is not cut out for business or life in the city. Early in the first act Biff expresses confusion as to why he has returned to the city, but suggests that one of the reasons may be his desire to take up a business career. He thinks that he is "like a boy," that he's "mixed up very bad," and that maybe he "oughta get stuck into something," and implies that this something could be business. Yet, although he decides to approach Oliver for money, he will not stay in the city but will use the money to buy a ranch in the West. By the end of the first act, however, Biff's confusion about going back West or staying in the city seems to have resolved itself in favor of the latter. An idea of Happy's about forming a water polo team excites him. And Biff, in Happy's words, begins to show the "old confidence" again. Biff can tell Happy, "I'm gonna go in to Oliver tomorrow and knock him for a—" and "steamed up: You know, with ten thousand bucks, boy!" This conviction carries through to the beginning of the second act. Linda reports that

> Biff was very changed this morning. His
> whole attitude seemed to be hopeful. He
> couldn't wait to get downtown to see Oliver.

Biff must feel he has an excellent chance with Oliver for he and Happy have offered to treat Willy to a big celebration meal that evening.

Both the reversal of Biff's goals and the beginning of his self-knowledge occur at Oliver's office. Oliver doesn't remember Biff and won't see him, and finally, after hours of waiting, Biff goes into Oliver's office, steals a golden fountain pen, and runs down eleven flights of stairs:

> And I suddenly stopped, you hear me? And
> in the middle of that office building, do
> you hear this? I stopped in the middle of
> that building and I saw—the sky. I saw the
> things that I love in this world. The work
> and the food and the time to sit and smoke.

38

                    And I looked at the pen and said to myself,
                    what the hell am I grabbing this for? Why
                    am I trying to become what I don't want to
                    be?

When Biff tells Willy, then, that "Today I realized something
about myself. . . ," part of what he is saying is that he has
discovered that "all I want is out there [in the West], waiting
for me. . . ." He has realized that he is not ambitious, is
not cut out for the competitiveness of business, that he is "not
a leader of men," that he is "A buck an hour!" And, therefore,
rather than stay in the city, he has made the decision to go
back out West and continue, presumably, to work on a ranch.
Thus in the Requiem he asks his brother, "Why don't you come
with me, Happy?" And when Happy defiantly says that he is
going to stay in the city to continue Willy's fight, Biff turns
away from Happy "with a hopeless glance."

        It would be pleasant to agree with those who find Biff a
tragic hero, especially since Biff is such a sympathetic and
likable person, and also since our need to find something
positive in the play evidently remains strong. Nevertheless we
may ask if Biff's decision to go back out West is based on self-
knowledge or on self-delusion. After all, life out West has
been no panacea for Biff in the past. True, he paints a pretty
picture for Happy of the West in the springtime, but that
Biff was never able to hold one job for very long. He drifted
from Nebraska to North and South Dakota, to Arizona and to
Texas; he continued his lifetime pattern of stealing (he explains in the second act that he has stolen himself out of every
job since high school); and at least once a year developed
severe enough anxiety that he came running home. At the end of
the play Biff makes a decision to reject the life of business
and the city with all of its obnoxious values as personified in
Willy, but he has obviously made that decision many times before.
Why are we to think this time is any different? Has, in fact,
anything different happened? What is to say that Biff won't
just go back to his old patterns of drifting, stealing, suffering from cycles of anxiety, and running home?[1]

                                II

        To answer this question we must try to understand why Biff
left home originally and what he was trying to find in the West.
Or, to turn the question around slightly, we must try to understand why Biff gave up a chance to go to the University of
Virginia on an athletic scholarship and presumably prepare

                                39

himself for a successful life in business. The turning point in Biff's life is easy to locate. During the last semester of his senior year in high school, Biff flunked math. In an attempt to get the grade turned around, Biff went to Boston hoping to convince his father to come home and talk to his teacher. Unfortunately for Biff, the evening he picked to arrive in Boston was one in which Willy was entertaining a lady in his hotel room. While Biff was talking to Willy, the lady, only partially dressed, came out of the bathroom while Biff stared at her "open mouthed and horrified." Bernard recounts that after Biff came back from Boston he

> took his sneakers--remember those sneakers
> with "University of Virginia" printed on
> them? He was so proud of those, wore them
> every day. And he took them down to the
> cellar, and burned them up in the furnace. . . .
> I've often thought how strange it was that I
> knew he'd given up his life.

Yet, if it is clear that this was the critical moment in Biff's relationship with his father, we still don't know why it was so decisive. In the flow of the play, especially as seen through Willy's hallucination, it seems natural that Biff's discovery should end in his throwing his life away. But it is important to remember that Biff's reaction may be viewed as rather extreme. As Ganz says:

> When Biff finds Willy with a prostitute, he at
> once concludes that his father's total view of
> life is erroneous, that his character is worth-
> less, and that he, Biff, is irretrievably lost--
> but why should he? His father's actions do not
> justify Biff's conclusions. Willy says in
> extenuation that he was lonely and the woman
> meant nothing to him. Biff, himself, we are
> told, has cut a considerable swath among the
> high school girls. Sons less devoted have for-
> given their fathers more [1963, p. 227].

Biff not only did not forgive Willy at that time, but in the years that have followed he still has not forgiven him. He makes hidden references to that event during the course of the play--and the event occurred seventeen years ago. Biff's intense reaction seems more logical if we theorize that as a boy he harbored intense anger toward his father. He needed to find a way to avenge himself upon Willy. I suggest that Biff used the Boston incident as an excuse to accomplish that end.[2]

Assuming the above theory to be correct, why would the young Biff be angry at Willy? This is a particularly important question

to ask because if we can believe the evidence in Willy's
hallucinations, Willy almost doted on Biff. Willy appears proud
of both sons, but he directs by far the most attention toward
Biff. Willy doesn't care about how Happy manages his girl-
friends, but cautions, "Just wanna be careful with those girls,
Biff, that's all." Both boys are cleaning the car, but Willy
thinks Happy is inept. "Show him how to do it, Biff." When
Willy decides the branch above the house has to be cut, he
addresses his remarks to Biff, not Happy:

>   Biff, first thing we gotta do when we get
>   time is clip that big branch over the house.

When Willy thinks about putting up a hammock between two trees,
again it is to Biff he directs the remark, not Happy:

>   Biff, up in Albany I saw a beautiful hammock.
>   I think I'll buy it next trip. . . .

Again if we can trust the material in Willy's hallucination,
despite all the attention Biff receives from Willy, and even
though it is obvious that Willy prefers Biff to Happy, Biff
competes with Happy for Willy's affection. Whenever Happy
manages to get Willy's attention focused on him, Biff fights to
get it back for himself. For example, in the excitement of
receiving the gift of the punching bag, Happy lies down on his
back, pedals with his feet and says, "I'm losing weight, you
notice, Pop?" And Willy does notice: "Jumping rope is good,
too." Biff immediately tries to bring the conversation around
to himself. He announces, "Did you see the new football I got?"
He succeeds in getting Willy's attention, for Willy takes the
ball and starts turning it over: "Where'd you get the new ball?"
Soon Willy is laughing with Biff about Biff's theft of the ball.
Happy is angry about being cut out of the conversation and when
he gets the opportunity he tells Biff that the coach will be
angry at Biff for stealing the ball. But Willy sides with Biff:
"Coach will probably congratulate you on your initiative!" Therefore, when Willy starts bragging about setting up his own
business, Happy makes an unkind comparison between Willy and
Charlie. Willy is stung, and turns defensive. Willy claims he
will be

>   Bigger than Uncle Charlie. Because Charlie
>   is not--liked. He's liked, but he's not--
>   well liked.

In his defensiveness, Willy is paying attention to what Happy
has said, so Biff immediately tries to pull Willy's attention
away. "Where'd you go this time, Dad?" And this opening allows
Willy to forget about Happy's remark and start talking about
his trip north. Even though Biff says, "Gee, I'd love to go with

you sometime, Dad," Willy starts talking about taking <u>both</u> Biff and Happy up north:

> Oh, won't that be something! Me comin' into the Boston stores with you boys carryin' my bags.

Biff cannot allow his father's favors to be shared in this way, so he starts "<u>prancing</u> <u>around</u>, <u>practicing</u> <u>passing</u> <u>the</u> <u>ball</u>." And this gambit succeeds in capturing his father's attention:

> Willy: You nervous, Biff, about the game?
>
> Biff: Not if you're gonna be there.

In fact, Biff <u>takes</u> <u>his</u> <u>father's</u> <u>hand</u> and promises that just for Willy he's "going to break through for a touchdown." Upset at Biff's getting Willy's attention, Happy criticizes Biff: "You're supposed to pass." Biff is having none of that:

> I'm takin' one play for Pop. You watch me, Pop, and when I take off my helmet, that means I'm breakin' out. Then you watch me crash through that line!

Biff has been completely successful in getting his father away from Happy for Willy <u>kisses</u> <u>Biff</u>.

All this provides a clue that there is something wrong in Biff's relationship with his father. Since Willy so obviously prefers Biff to Happy, why does Biff feel it necessary to fight with Happy for Willy's love?

The answer to this question requires a discussion of what it is that a boy needs from his father. Obviously, this is a complex topic, but some generalizations can be made that are important to our study of Biff. Boys are destined, after all, to grow into men. Part of the condition of boyhood is not only an attraction to the pleasures and privileges of becoming a man, but also a terror at the prospects of adulthood. Any boy is afraid to one degree or another that he will not be able to compete successfully with other men and win a suitable position and woman in the world's struggle. In an attempt to alleviate these fears a young boy will look to his father for help. His father, hopefully, has succeeded in professional or social competition and in a relationship with a woman. As the boy views the father, the father is strong, the father has manhood. Emulating his father, the boy tries to draw strength from him. While trying to become his father, the boy works for his father's love and approval.

Superficially it might appear that Willy has made a good model for Biff. He certainly brags enough around his boys about how successful he has been in business, and there are no obvious flaws in his relationship with Linda. Yet even a superficial analysis of Willy's character shows that he feels inadequate around older men. He swings between idealizing anyone of whom he approves (Ben, Old Man Wagner, Dave Singleman, Bill Oliver) and attacking anyone who doesn't measure up to his inflated standards (most notably Charlie). He explains that he has felt rather "temporary" about himself ever since his own father left for Alaska; the way he hangs on Ben's advice and brags about his own questionable business successes is pathetic. Clearly Willy hopes that Biff will remedy his feelings of inadequacy. Biff will be a great football star and a magnificent businessman. By identifying with Biff, Willy can forget his own failures and include himself in Biff's successes. True, Willy flatters Biff and builds him up, but there is both a threat and a price in that flattery. In order to deserve it, Biff must be the strong and successful adult with whom Willy can identify. It is a vicious circle, for in order to receive from his father the love and strength he so desperately needs, Biff must demonstrate to Willy that he, Biff, already is an adult.

What happens when a boy's father turns to his son for the same strength, love, and approval that the boy seeks from his father? The reaction may take many forms, of course, but a common pattern is for the son to choose to fail. Failure fulfills, in a neurotic and unproductive way, two deep needs of the son: 1) to hurt his father for not having given his strength and love, and 2) to force his father to come rescue him. This mechanism will operate especially strongly whenever the pressure on the son to succeed as an adult is the strongest.

The Boston incident becomes more understandable when we consider Biff's need to fail in reaction to Willy's demands on him. On the surface it appears that Biff goes to Boston because he wants his father's help getting into the University of Virginia. But we must remember when this incident happened: at the time Biff was about to graduate, at the time he was expected to go out into the world and succeed as an adult. It would be at this time that his fear of failure would be greatest and therefore his anger at his father strongest. Biff's flunking math is certainly suspect. As far as we know, this is the first subject he has ever flunked; more importantly, he must have done fairly well on the Regents (or some other similar type of test) to get into a school of the quality of the University of Virginia. We suspect that Biff flunked math in order to hurt his father, and that his real purpose in going to Boston was to hurt Willy with the news of his failure, not to seek his help: his first words to Willy are, "Dad--I let you

down." Of course Biff cannot admit this to himself. He must
consciously think he is seeking his father's help. But if this
were his real motive he would have surely ignored, or at least
not attached as much importance to, finding his father with the
woman. He might have been shocked, but in his urgent need to
get his father back to New York he would have somehow ignored
her. But the suddenness with which he drops his plans to have
his father help him ("He [the math teacher] wouldn't listen to
you") and the quickness with which he announces he will not go
to the University of Virginia reveal his true motives. He
seizes the opportunity to hurt his father by implying that due
to weakness in his father's character, Biff's failure is his
father's fault. He is able to call his father a "liar," and
charges him:

> You fake! You phony little fake! You fake!

This is projection. It is Biff at this point who is the liar
and the phony little fake. And in any case, if Biff really
wanted to go to the University of Virginia, even supposing he
had really been disillusioned by his father's behavior, he
could have gone to summer school and made up math. But, as the
adult Bernard says,

> I've often thought of how strange it was that
> I knew he'd given up his life [when he returned
> from Boston].

III

Not only has Biff attempted to hurt Willy because of his
fear of failure in the past, but he also indulges in the same
pattern of behavior during the course of the play. In order to
demonstrate this pattern, we should quickly review, from the
point of view of Biff, how the play is constructed. After
some amount of confusion in the first act, Biff allows himself
to hope that he may succeed in business (the water polo idea) by
getting a loan from Oliver. At the beginning of the second act
his hopes are still very high. But he does not get the loan and
Oliver treats him in such a manner that Biff realizes what a
failure and phony he is, "what a lie my life has been."
Oliver's rejection, in fact, has a stunning impact on Biff. He
can tell Happy, "I'm all numb, I swear," and he talks about
what happened in Oliver's office "<u>with</u> <u>great</u> <u>tension</u> <u>and</u> <u>wonder</u>."
After having evaluated Biff's past we can see that this event
repeats a chronic problem for Biff: the surfacing of the knowledge that he is not a man, that he is a failure. And once

again, as with the Boston incident when Biff went to his father's hotel to confront Willy, Biff now has an urgent need to see Willy. When Biff comes into the restaurant he tells Happy,

> Now look, I want to tell Dad a couple of
> things, and I want you to help me.

He wants to confront his father with the fact that he, Biff, didn't get the loan from Oliver and that he, Biff, is a failure. In the flow of the play it appears to us as quite natural that Biff should wish to tell his father these things. But Biff might have handled things quite differently. After all, Willy's emotional condition is at the least precarious. Biff knows very well that Willy's life is in danger. He has personally inspected the hose and gas set-up in the basement, and, indeed, is carrying the hose with him now. If the experience with Oliver has made him realize some painful but important things about himself, that is fine. But considering Willy's unsettled condition, why must he tell Willy? Can't he engage in some white lies? Can't he string Willy along as Happy suggests? He could, but Biff has been made to feel a failure at Oliver's. He is enraged and must strike back. He acts out his old pattern of hurting his father by flaunting his, Biff's, failure in his father's face. He formulates all this to himself in such a way that he does not have to admit his real motives. Rather he makes it seem as if he were trying to help Willy:

> Hap, he's [Willy's] got to understand that
> I'm not the man somebody lends that kind of
> money to. He thinks I've been spiting him
> all these years and it's eating him up.

The defense is almost perfect: I am going to hurt Willy by telling him I am a failure, but the reason I am going to hurt him is to show him I have not been hurting him. Willy's reaction on hearing Biff's news is immediately defensive, but Biff is so enraged by what happened at Oliver's that he keeps pressing and finally manages to get out all the "facts and aspects":

> at the table, now audible, holding up a gold
> fountain pen:. . . so I'm washed up with
> Oliver, you understand?

He insults his father ("Look at you! Look at what's become of you!"), and turns away from his father when the girls arrive:

> ignoring Willy: How're you, Miss, sit down.
> What do you drink?

Willy, in an extremely disassociative state, finds his way to the bathroom, and Biff lets him go. Of course, Biff defends his actions by projecting his own guilt on Happy:

> Biff: Why don't you do something for him?
>
> Happy: Me!
>
> Biff: Don't you give a damn for him, Hap?
>
> Happy: What're you talking about? I'm the one who--
>
> Biff: I sense it, you don't give a good goddam about him.

We can tell that Biff knows his own actions may kill Willy since he "takes the rolled-up hose from his pocket" and places it in front of Happy. Again he projects his guilty feelings on Happy:

> Look what I found in the cellar, for Christ's sake. How can you bear to let it go on?. . . He's going to kill himself, don't you know that?

The above analysis is unfair in one sense: Biff's entire motivation does not appear to be anger at his father. He also seems to be attempting to tell his father something truthful about himself--that he is a failure, that he needs his father's understanding, strength, and help. In this sense Biff is acting out his other deep-seated behavioral pattern, but one that is very hidden: an attempt to get his father to rescue him. He has tried to get another father figure (Oliver) to give him strength in the form of money, and failing that, if he can show Willy he is nothing, surely he can win his father's support and strength. We see this deeply hidden need in his last line to Happy:

> Hap, help him [Willy]. . . . Help him. . . . Help me, help me. . . .

Here Biff confuses himself with Willy. And "ready to weep, he hurries out," forcing Happy and the girls to follow him.

If Biff is determined to have a confrontation with Willy
in the restaurant after his humiliation at Oliver's office, he
is even more determined to do so after he arrives home. Linda
sees danger and tries to block him:

> Linda: Get out of here!
>
> Biff: I gotta talk to the boss, Mom. Where
> is he?
>
> Linda: You're not going near him. Get out
> of the house.
>
> Biff, with absolute assurance, determination:
> No. We're gonna have an abrupt conversation,
> him and me.

What is appalling about Biff's behavior is that by confronting
Willy now, Biff most seriously endangers Willy's life. As
Linda says, "violently to Biff: Don't you care whether he lives
or dies?" But this prospect doesn't seem to concern Biff:

> What do you mean, lives or dies? Nobody's
> dying around here, pal.

Biff doesn't heed Linda's warning because of the same
motives we have discussed above. On the one hand, he is still
so enraged by his failure with Oliver that he must act out his
anger; on the other hand, he is even more desperate to receive
his father's support and strength. We see these contradictory
emotions most clearly in the final confrontation. The stage
directions reveal the rage:

> Biff starts for Willy, but is blocked by
> Happy. In his fury, Biff seems on the
> verge of attacking his father.

Again,

> Biff breaks from Happy. Willy, in fright,
> starts up the stairs. Biff grabs him.

Paradoxically, yet logically enough, Biff's language belies
his physical rage. Biff shouts to his father that he is not
strong, that he is weak and impotent, that he's "a buck an
hour," and that he couldn't "raise it." We see the contradiction most blatantly between action and words when Biff

47

breaks from Happy, starts up the stairs and grabs hold of Willy.

> at the peak of his fury: Pop, I'm nothing!
> I'm nothing, Pop. Can't you understand that?

Yet, as we have seen, the words have a strong aggressive component. Biff attempts to hurt Willy by flaunting his, Biff's, failure. Willy is defensive:

> I won't take the rap for this, you hear?
>
> . . . .
>
> I suppose that's my fault.
>
> . . . .
>
> You vengeful, spiteful mut!

Yet, contradictorily again, there is another message that comes through these words: Biff is helpless and needs help. He is nothing and wants his father to keep him from being nothing and to give him strength. We see this hidden desire come out most dramatically in Biff's actions after his paroxysm of rage:

> Biff's fury has spent itself, and he breaks
> down, sobbing, holding on to Willy, who
> dumbly fumbles for Biff's face.

Here is the child, crying, broken, seeking comfort. It is a brief moment, but telling.

V

Biff claims that he has learned something about himself, that he now knows who he is. Yet the compulsion that drives him to attack his father and at the same time seek his strength negates this claim. Biff may in fact lay some truths about himself and his family out in the open, but he has no comprehension at all of his motivations for doing so. The most telling demonstration that Biff does not know himself occurs during the Requiem when Biff does not admit to any responsibility for Willy's death but rather places the blame on Willy:

> He had the wrong dreams, all wrong.
>
> . . . .

He never knew who he was.

When Charlie tries to put some perspective on Willy's way of life ("A salesman is got to dream, boy"), Biff rejects it: "Charlie, the man didn't know who he was." Biff's claim to Happy, "I know who I am, kid," is pure self-deception. Biff will go back out West, but because he has been unable to avoid acting out old patterns at home, he will probably continue as a drifter and a failure, stealing from time to time, and intermittently rushing home to find those things that are now forever lost.

Chapter III

WILLY

I

        Even those who have argued that Biff qualifies as the
tragic hero of Death of a Salesman agree the play is written
in such a way that audiences identify not with Biff, but with
Willy. The strength and depth of that identification has been
a source of endless confusion for the critics. Willy, simply,
should not attract such attention. If we were to meet him in
real life we would probably ignore him, and it is doubtful
that we would like him. Gassner calls Willy a "loud-mouthed
dolt and emotional babe in the woods. . . ," and complains that
playwrights like Moliere and Shaw would have held him up for
ridicule [1954, p. 368]. Many critics have been at pains to
point out that Willy does not have the stature or greatness to
command our respect.[1] He is (to use Miller's own phrase) a
"common man" who learns nothing, going to his death believing
in the very ideals which betrayed him. Why, then, do we follow
his actions with such intensity? Why are we so fascinated with
him?

        Death of a Salesman centers on suicide. That is the heart
of the play. We meet a Willy who has been powerfully drawn
toward taking his life for some time (the car accidents, the
device in the cellar), and is now in the last and most
desperate stages of his suicide. Yet it is surprising how
little attention previous writers have given to this central
action. It is almost as if they believed Miller had tacked
on the suicide as something extra, something not really in-
tegral to the drama, a convenient and perhaps even dishonest
way to play on our emotions. But more than anything, Willy's
loosening grip on his sanity is the play. He may be an
adolescent and self-pitying man, but we share his inner terrors--
whether we are aware of them or not. We follow Willy's
struggle with fascination. It is this struggle which makes
him universal, for we are in danger, too. The demon of suicide
lies within us, waiting. We are drawn to this solution more

51

passionately than we know. Our defenses against it remain tenuous. The tragic hero has always been one who is less and less able to defend against powerful and unacceptable needs within himself and is in greater and greater danger of being overwhelmed by them. He is finally driven to take one last desperate and insane action, no matter what its cost, to avoid a confrontation with himself. The tragic poet is able to involve his audiences in a deep identification with the process of the hero's struggle. The poet binds us to danger, too. It is from the reality of this danger that Death of a Salesman draws its primary power. As Withim points out,

> The more purely, the more completely, a work
> confronts its reader with his potential
> destruction, the more purely and completely
> is that a work of tragedy [1973, p. 497].

Miller has offered a number of clues to the emotions behind Willy's final action. Yet since Willy's feelings are so hidden from his consciousness (and ours--thus the lack of critical comment on the subject), they are not going to be easy to identify. Miller has drawn a complex and protective maze around them. We will have to work through this maze slowly and inferentially.

Many writers have concluded that Willy takes his final desperate action because of his realization that it is his only remaining way of giving something to his family, and especially to his son Biff.[2] Certainly this wish is one element in his suicide. Moreover, Biff's returning home and his violent quarrels with Willy are also related to Willy's death. But Willy would have committed suicide sooner or later anyway. He has had a number of car "accidents" and has rigged up a hose and nipple arrangement on a gas pipe in the cellar. More and more he has been hallucinating openly, talking so that others can hear him, reliving or inventing scenes and people out of the past. As we watch him walking, exhausted, carrying his valises into the house, we know he is in the final stages of an emotional collapse. The forces of his unconscious are pushing through his weakening defenses and will soon overwhelm him. But why? And why does this approaching collapse take the form of suicide? What is it about death that so attracts him? How can anyone be attracted to something so horrible?

Part of the problem of attempting to answer these questions is the use of the abstract term "death." To say that Willy is attracted to "death" is to say almost nothing since that word is so intellectualized, so removed from the reality it is supposed to describe. Willy, in fact, never once uses the word "death" in connection with his suicide, nor does he understand his last desperate action as the end of something. Rather he views it as a beginning. He understands himself to be starting a trip to gain treasure. At the end of the play as he is preparing for suicide, he imagines he is talking to his older brother, Ben. Ben, so he imagines, has returned from Alaska and is now about to board a boat headed for the continent of Africa where Ben made his fortune in diamonds. Ben beckons Willy toward the African jungle and its diamonds:

> The jungle is dark but full of diamonds, Willy.
>
> . . . .
>
> One must go in to fetch a diamond out.
>
> . . . .
>
> It's dark there, but full of diamonds.

Willy's view of death as a kind of trip to Africa helps us begin to understand his motivation, for not only are the images of "Africa," the "jungle," and "diamonds" more concrete than the word, "death," but they are part of a whole pattern of images in the play.

Miller has incorporated a pun into his protagonist's name: "low man." As many writers have pointed out, Willy is a "low man" most obviously in the sense that he has been a small and insignificant failure. This pun is not isolated. A whole pattern of imagery associates lowness with career failure and highness with career success. Willy for example, has always had the fondest dreams that Biff would become a success in life. In a flashback he tells Ben that three great universities are begging for Biff, "and from there the sky's the limit," and he fondly recalls that "When that team came out—he was the tallest." But Biff flunked math and Willy, remembering the time, tells Bernard, "He flunked the subject and he laid down and died like a hammer hit him." Willy refuses to take any blame for what happened to Biff. Rather, Willy tells him that "you cut down your life for spite," and that "when you're down and out remember what did it."

In a sense both boys have tried to be successful. Happy has been struggling to show the other executives that "he can make the grade," and Biff spent six or seven years "trying to work myself up" after high school. But now Biff has a new plan for success. Oliver will help him. Willy is excited by the idea since "If he'd stayed with Oliver he'd be on top now." And he cautions Biff, "Don't stoop." The important thing is not to be modest. "You always started too low. . . ." But Biff's plans don't work out. Oliver won't see him, and in an irrational fit of anger Biff steals Oliver's fountain pen and, in this moment of defeat, runs "down all eleven flights."

According to Linda, Old Man Wagner may have once told Willy, "if he keeps it up he'll be a member of the firm," but in fact Willy's real life circumstances are powerfully pictured for us at the opening of the play. An exhausted man, unable to drive any more, he lugs his valises toward a fragile seeming house which is at the bottom of a vault of "towering" apartment houses. The house is so far down the sun hardly reaches it any more ("you can't raise a carrot in the back yard"), and you "Gotta break your neck to see a star in this yard."

In a geographical sense as well, "highness" is associated with career success and "lowness" with career failure. Whatever career success Willy has had or has fantasized he might have had, has been north of New York City. Willy is a road man, and it is important that the direction he travels is north to New England. At the beginning of the play when Willy is obviously tired and exhausted and unable to drive any more, Linda suggests that Willy "go down to the place tomorrow and tell Howard" he's got to have a place in the home store. But Willy does not feel comfortable "down" in New York:

> They don't need me in New York. I'm the
> New England man. I'm vital in New England.

In the first flashback as Willy brags to his sons about his business prowess, he relates how he went to a group of northern cities, from south to north. He started in Providence (where he had coffee with the mayor), to Waterbury ("Sold a nice bill there"), to Boston, "and on to Portland and Bangor." Willy claims he is so successful and well known up north that "I can park my car in any street in New England, and the cops protect it like their own." He tells his sons of the "beautiful towns and [the] fine, upstanding people," and suggests that "when I bring you fellas up, they'll be open sesame for all of us. . . ." And he can tell Linda, "it's so beautiful up there."

Of course, we know that actually Willy has never been that successful and that "northerness" has not, in reality, any connection with his success. He has not, to use his own word,

been "vital" in New England. Nevertheless, Willy often thinks
that if he had his life to live over, he would have gone even
further north and found success in Alaska:

> Because in those days I had a yearning to go
> to Alaska. . . . Oh, yeah, my father lived many
> years in Alaska. He was an adventurous man.
> We've got quite a little streak of self-
> reliance in our family. I thought I'd go out
> with my older brother and try and locate him,
> and maybe settle in the north with my old man.

Now, in his later years, he regrets that decision not to go: "If
I'd gone with him [Ben] to Alaska that time, everything would
have been totally different." As he asks Happy, "Why didn't I
go with my brother Ben that time! . . . He begged me to go."

Miller draws our attention to Willy's attraction to Alaska
in another way. During the first act of the play, Ben, Willy's
older brother, drops by, as it were, on his way north to Alaska
("I must make a train, William. There are several properties
I'm looking at in Alaska"). Of course, the Ben we meet in the
play is not the real Ben (who died before the play opens). In
his state of near emotional collapse Willy often hallucinates,
or, if one prefers, openly dreams, and during a visit from his
neighbor, Charlie, he invents a figure "Ben" who continues to
"visit" and "advise" Willy. Ben, as a figment of Willy's
imagination, is a projection of Willy's unconscious needs. The
advice Ben gives is really advice Willy is giving to himself.
And therefore it is no surprise when Ben dwells on the qualities
of Alaska and wonders why Willy has not gone there: "Opportunity
is tremendous in Alaska, William. Surprised you're not there."
Willy has Ben buy land in Alaska and suggest that Willy go north
and take care of it:

> You've a new continent at your doorstep,
> William. Get out of these cities, they're full
> of talk and time payments and courts of law.
> Screw on your fists and you can fight for a
> fortune up there.

This advice to himself is symbolic and not practical. Any idea
of Willy's actually going to Alaska (to seek his fortune) is
at his age and in his emotional state out of the question. But
Ben's "advice" shows how powerfully "up" symbolizes certain of
Willy's unconscious needs, which are here represented by "north"
and "Alaska."

Ben's appearance and advice also illustrate a paradox in
Willy's struggle. Willy has Ben traveling to Alaska to make some
investments, but Ben does not live in Alaska, nor is he generally

associated with it. He is going north on a temporary trip, and in the second act of the play he reverses directions and drops by to see Willy on his way back to his real home in Africa. Not only does Ben live in Africa, but more importantly, Ben emphasizes that it was in the African jungles that he made his huge fortune:

> William, when I walked into the jungle, I was seventeen. When I walked out I was twenty-one. And, by God, I was rich.

At the end of the play, Willy attempts to follow Ben not to the timberland of Alaska, but south to the jungles of Africa.

There are certain similarities between Alaska and Africa: their names sound somewhat the same and both are covered by trees (Ben tells Willy he's bought "timberland in Alaska" and the "jungle is dark" because of the matting of trees). But obviously there are very important distinctions between Alaska and Africa: one is "up" and "north" and one is "down" and "south." (Africa may not be in a direct line south of North America, but Ben says that instead of going north to Alaska, he walked south and arrived in Africa.) On the most obvious level Alaska should suggest career success and Africa career failure. But Willy knows no one who has made money in Alaska. And since Ben, who is the most successful man Willy knows, made his fortune in Africa, we must be alerted to the possibility that for Willy "down" and "south" suggest success. And this in turn poses the question: how can Willy be attracted to two different "directions" at once?

A helpful key to answering this question can be found by inspecting another important image pattern in the play which is closely woven in to the imagery of "highness," "lowness," "Alaska," and "Africa": "gold" and "diamonds." Just as Alaska and Africa share certain similarities, gold and diamonds are similar in that they are precious and must be dug up from the ground. However, they are associated with two very different parts of the world: gold with Alaska and diamonds with Africa. Willy tells Howard he had a yearning to go to Alaska because "there were three gold strikes in one month" and it is "Principally diamond mines" in which Ben made his fortune in Africa. Since gold is thereby associated with "up" and "north," we would also expect it to be associated with career success, and it is. One of the ways Willy is able to keep some optimism in life is by believing that Biff will be a great success, and Biff as a success is often associated with gold. When Willy and Linda remember the all-city championship football game, Linda describes Biff as having been "in gold." Willy picks up the theme: "And the sun, the sun all around him." At the same time, Biff comes "downstage into a golden pool of light." Later, in Willy's fantasy of preparing to go to the game, an argument develops over who will get the honor of carrying Biff's <u>helmet</u>. Miller tells us the color of that helmet, but not the color of the rest of his uniform. "Happy carries Biff's shoulder guards, <u>gold</u> helmet, and football pants." Happy and Bernard fight over the helmet:

> Bernard: Biff, I'm carrying your helmet, aren't I?
>
> Happy: No, I'm carrying the helmet.
>
> Bernard: No, Biff you promised me.
>
> Happy: I'm carrying the helmet.

Biff tells Willy, "And remember, pal, when I take off my <u>helmet</u>, that touchdown is for you."

However, gold is not always associated with success. Willy can tell Howard that his father went to Alaska in search of gold, but if he ever found any, Willy is unaware of it. The preparations for the "big game" may be strongly associated with gold, but it is significant that Miller supplies us with no evidence about what happened at the game. The oversight is strange since this time represents for Willy the height of Biff's success. Willy remembers all the details of the glory up to the start of the game:

> Remember how he waved to me? Right up from the field, with the representatives of three colleges standing by? And the buyers I brought, and the cheers when he came out--Loman, Loman, Loman!

But since Willy remembers nothing <u>of</u> the game or its final score, we are entitled to wonder if Biff, even with his golden helmet, was on the losing side. Such an assumption is further strengthened by the fact that at another important point in Biff's and Willy's struggles, gold is connected to failure. Biff's great hope during the course of the play is to get Oliver to help set him up in business. Biff goes to his office, and after waiting for him a full day, finally sees him for only one minute. In this moment of defeat and despair, Biff goes into Oliver's office and steals a <u>gold</u> fountain pen and runs "<u>down</u> eleven flights" of stairs. As a result of his meeting with Oliver, when Biff is trying desperately to explain to Willy that he is a failure, he displays "a <u>gold</u> fountain pen."

Gold is associated with failure in another way. Its very color is related to the orange, yellow and red colors of fire, and the images of fire in the play are associated with failure.

For example, at the same time Biff is bathed in a pool of golden
light, Miller has him standing next to a gas heater in which we
see flames and red coils. The gas heater is connected with
one form of Willy's suicide attempt, and the redness of the coils
remind us of the apartment houses which tower above Willy and
are lit in an "angry glow of orange." The area above and around
Willy seems to be ablaze--which is surely Miller's intention,
since when Willy meets his greatest humiliation and failure,
being taken off the job by Howard, he tells Biff and Happy,

> the woods are burning, boys, you understand?
> There's a big blaze going all around. I was
> fired today.

And when Biff flunked math, thus, according to Willy, ruining
Biff's career, the name of the teacher who flunked him
phonetically reminds us of fire: Birnbaum. This name points
to yet another association. Since baum in German means tree, the
teacher's whole name can be related to Willy's remark about
burning trees: "the woods are burning."

Although gold may not always be associated with success,
diamonds always are. When Willy hears Ben has made his fortune
in Africa he exclaims, "The Gold Coast." But Ben corrects him:
"Principally diamond mines." At the end of the play when Willy
has decided finally to follow Ben into the jungle, it is not
gold he hopes to find there, but diamonds:

> Oh, Ben, that's the whole beauty of it! I
> see it like a diamond, shining in the
> dark. . . .

And Ben, who we know is just a projection of Willy's own desires,
agrees: "The jungle is dark but full of diamonds, Willy."

The whole pattern doesn't seem to make sense. Superficially
the imagery is clear: highness suggests success, and lowness
suggests failure. Willy appears to strive for highness and
avoid lowness. As we have seen, however, the qualities associated with highness, the direction north, Alaska and gold, are
not always associated with success; whereas the qualities connected with lowness, the direction south, Africa and diamonds,
are. In the final analysis, Willy seems much more attracted to
south, Africa and diamonds than he is to north, Alaska and gold.

This apparent confusion must mirror a similar confusion in
Willy's emotional make-up. On the deepest level Willy is
passionately attracted to "lowness." But such an attraction is
inadmissible to his view of himself. In his conscious mind he
sees himself as one who is striving for "highness." Since
these two needs are contradictory, he solves the problem by

58

hiding the qualities of "lowness" in the qualities of "highness."
The one stands as a screen for the other. Therefore, by
striving for "highness," he can actually be attaining "lowness."
While going in one direction, magically, he can go in the other.

Ben, as we might expect, is the model for this magical
reversal of direction. Willy is never really sure how Ben
gained his success. But he thinks, as he tells Happy, he should
have gone with Ben:

> Why didn't I go to _Alaska_ with my brother
> Ben that time! That man was a genius,
> that man was success incarnate! What a
> mistake! He begged me to go.

Yet Ben did not end up in Alaska (which is associated with highness), but in Africa (which is associated with lowness). How
this happened is central to an understanding of Willy:

> Willy: How did you get started?
>
> Ben: Well, I don't know how much you
> remember. . . .
>
> Willy: I remember you walking down some
> open road.
>
> Ben, _laughing_: I was going to find Father
> in Alaska.
>
> Willy: Where is he?
>
> Ben: At that age I had a very faulty view
> of geography, William. I discovered after
> a few days that I was heading due south, so
> instead of Alaska, I ended up in Africa.

Although Miller makes it clear in his stage directions that Ben
has an aura around him of someone who is absolutely certain of
his destiny, what is significant here is that it was not Ben's
utter certainty that got him to Africa, but his ignorance and
innocence. He was confidently heading one way and magically
ended up going the other. He arrived at the jungle by
"accident." He did not "intend" to. Thus when Willy hears
about Ben's success and exclaims to his sons, "You see what I'm
talking about? The greatest things can happen," he is not only
referring to Ben's walk in and out of the jungle, but to the
fact that Ben didn't _intend_ to go to Africa. By consciously
striving after highness, maybe Willy, too can "accidentally" get
what he really wants.

At the all-city championship football game, we find "lowness" hidden once again in "highness." Although the game
is strongly associated with gold, Willy's major hallucination
about preparations for the game emphasizes details which lead
us to doubt that Biff is the successful football "golden boy."
Surely, since this is a creative work, Miller had the choice
of tens of fields in New York City where he might have placed
the game. But he puts it in Ebbets Field, which is a baseball
field. We might not attach much importance to the matter
except that Miller is at pains to emphasize the confusion by
having the boys argue about football and baseball terminology.
Bernard wants to carry something "Cause I told everyone I'm
going to be in the locker room." But Happy points out, "In
Ebbets Field it's the clubhouse." And Bernard quickly agrees,
"I meant the clubhouse, Biff." Charlie teases Willy by pre-
tending that Biff is going to play baseball and not football.
When Linda says Biff is playing in Ebbets Field, Charlie replies,
"Baseball in this weather?" And as Biff leaves, Charlie calls
after him, "Knock a homer, Biff, knock a homer!" Why the confusion? Because Willy is not really attracted to football but
to its opposite, here symbolized by baseball. Later the woman
in Boston, whose dialogue Willy also invents, will ask Biff,
who has failed, if he is football or baseball. It is probably
too ingenious to suggest that baseball is associated with
baseball "diamonds," yet at the end of the first act when Willy
is in bed and remembering the day of the game and how Biff was
the tallest with "the sun, the sun all around him," he manages
to combine his description with diamond imagery--changing the
emphasis from the sun to a star:

> God Almighty, he'll be great yet. A <u>star</u>
> like that, magnificent, can never really
> fade away.

The word "magnificent," which is here applied to both Biff and
a star, is repeated by Willy at the end of the second act:
"That boy--that boy is going to be magnificent!" And the star
that Willy says would never fade away is seen in the dark in
the form of a diamond: "Oh, Ben, that's the whole beauty of it!
I see it like a diamond shining in the dark."

As the play progresses and Willy's emotional state increasingly disintegrates, his defenses against realizing his
hidden wishes for "down" become weaker and weaker. This dis-
solution of his defenses is pictured partly through the change
of direction Ben makes during the play. In the first act Ben
is heading north; in the second act, he is heading south. When
Ben first arrives he has several properties he's looking at in
Alaska and has just dropped by before his "appointment in
Ketchikan Tuesday week." By the second act we know he has been
to Alaska since Willy asks, "Did you wind up the Alaska deal

already?" and Ben replies,

> Doesn't take much time if you know what
> you're doing. Just a short business trip.
> Boarding ship in an hour.

The ship he is boarding is going to Africa. Of course, it is
true that in the first act of the play, and even in the first
part of the second act, Ben makes suggestions that Willy go
to Alaska, but by the end of the second act, Willy, through
Ben, has dropped all pretense of wishing to go north. "And
it does take a great kind of man to crack the jungle." Whereas
before Willy always had to associate Biff with "up" images, now
he can call out to Biff and stress "lowness":

> Now when you kick off, boy, I want a seventy-
> yard boot, and get right down under the ball,
> and when you hit, hit low and hit hard, because
> it's important, boy.

To Linda's repeated urgings, "I want you upstairs," "Come right
up," "Willy! Come up!", "Willy, you coming up?", Willy replies,
"I just want to settle down, Linda." Moments later he is dead.

III

"Down," "south," "Africa" and "diamonds" are not isolated
images in the play; they are closely interwoven with a pattern
of other images. The diamonds that Ben promises Willy inside
the jungle (not to mention the gold of Alaska) will be found in
the ground. Willy seems attracted to things in the ground. A
number of times he expresses a desire to plant seeds, and, as he
tells Stanley, the waiter, with considerable urgency, "I don't
have a thing in the ground." We can't help but associate "down"
with under the ground. And, of course, under the ground has
always been associated with death—if for no other reason than
that we bury the corpse there.

Another and more pervasive meaning associated with being
under the ground is a return to the womb. We refer to the earth
as Mother Earth, and all things underground are inside her. We
come from dust and return to dust. Not only does Ben describe
the jungle as dark, but as something one goes into. Suicide is
a way of following Ben inside ("And it does take a great kind of
man to crack the jungle"). Willy's strongest desire is to return to a condition he knew before he was born, a consummation
to be found in death. He understands his suicide, then, not as

a negative act of destroying himself, but as a positive act of
gaining a coveted existence. His wish to give his family, and
especially his son, Biff, a better life is real enough, but
this desire fades beside the power of his hunger for following
Ben. Willy may have Ben say that he, Ben, went into the jungle
when he was seventeen and came out when he was twenty-one; but
hearing this, Willy can exclaim, "To walk into the jungle! I
was right, I was right! I was right." He mentions nothing
about walking out again.

Willy's passion to return to the womb is demonstrated in
other ways. An adult has generally developed a strong sense of
ego. By contrast, a baby has no sense of "I," no sense of
self--that is, no ego. There is no borderline for him between
the unconscious and the conscious, between inside and outside.
As the infant grows toward childhood he is slowly able to
develop a conscious state which can hold itself free from the
unconscious for longer and longer periods of time. Slowly the
child is able to give more and more direction to his psychic
energies. Yet, in one sense, even in the adult the ego always
remains an artificial construct which must be constantly defended and reinforced and is never without danger of collapse.
Keppler has offered an interesting metaphor to describe that
precarious existence:

> The waking ego consciousness is no more than
> a small and lonely outpost of light whose
> knowledge of the vast dark hinterland of psychic
> energy from which it emerged is fragmentary
> and inferential [1972, p. 5].

Keppler's description reminds us of an untamed and uncharted
jungle, surrounding and ready to choke off a cleared area made
by man. The healthy adult is reasonably successful at keeping
the "jungle" at bay. But the man who wishes to return to the
womb does not wish to guard against the "jungle"; rather he
longs for it. Ben describes the jungle as dark because of the
heavy matting of trees. It should come as no surprise that
Willy longs for trees. Often when he hallucinates "the entire
house and surroundings become covered with leaves." Ben, who
came out of the trees of Africa, heads toward the trees of
Alaska. He can report to Willy that "I've bought timberland in
Alaska and I need a man to look after things for me." Willy,
hearing this, can respond, "God, timberland!" In the stench of
the city Willy remembers "those two beautiful elm trees," and
the swing he had between them. Willy thinks they "should've
arrested the builder for cutting those trees down." The flute
we hear at the beginning of the play tells of grass and trees.
Recently Willy has begun to look at trees more and more as he
drives out of the city. He tells his wife, "But it's beautiful
up there, Linda, the trees are so thick. . . ." Several times

when the hard facts of reality become too much for Willy, he can complain that these pleasant trees are being destroyed: "The woods are burning." And although Willy associates trees primarily with the state of unconsciousness to which he wishes to return, he uses other aspects of nature—flowers, nice smells, warmth, the sun, fresh air, and so forth—in the same way. For example:

> <u>Lost</u>: More and more I think of those days, Linda. This time of year it was lilac and wisteria. And the peonies would come out, and the daffodils. What a fragrance in this room.

Significantly, at the beginning of the play Willy discovers that he has lost the ability to drive a car. More accurately, he is no longer able to <u>control</u> it. It goes too fast; it goes off the road.

> No, it's me, it's me. Suddenly I realize I'm going sixty miles an hour and I don't remember the last five minutes. I'm—I can't seem to—keep my mind to it.

The ego is often symbolized by an object, like an automobile or ship, over which we exert conscious control and which we cause to move from place to place over a vast reach. A car moves across landscape, a ship through the sea. The concept of motion implies possible lack of motion. The car, the ship, may come to rest. The countryside and the ocean, which represent the unconscious, will always be there, waiting. They are indestructible. If control is not exerted over a car or a ship it may go off the road or become lost in the sea. Thus Willy's admission that he cannot drive represents his <u>loss</u> <u>of</u> <u>control</u>: "I suddenly couldn't drive any more. The <u>car</u> <u>kept</u> <u>going</u> <u>off</u> <u>the</u> <u>shoulder</u>, y'know?" This loss of ego control is most evident when Willy's thoughts are drawn to the natural objects which he associates with the pre-conscious, ego-less existence in the womb:

> I was driving along, you understand? And I was fine. I was even observing the <u>scenery</u>. You can imagine, me looking at the <u>scenery</u>, on the road every week of my life. But it's <u>so</u> <u>beautiful</u> up there, Linda, the <u>trees</u> are so <u>thick</u>, and the <u>sun</u> is <u>warm</u>. I opened the windshield and just let the <u>warm</u> <u>air</u> <u>bathe</u> <u>over</u> <u>me</u>. And then all of a sudden I'm <u>goin'</u> <u>off</u> <u>the</u> <u>road</u>! I'm tellin' ya, I absolutely forgot I was driving. . . . I have such thoughts, I have such strange thoughts.

Here it is specifically after he experiences his attraction to trees, flowers, and warmth that the loss of control occurs. He "absolutely forgot I was driving." That is, he loses consciousness, loses control, and the car, the ego, goes "off the road" into the vastness of "such strange thoughts."

Just as one side of Willy longs for the jungle, another side of him is terrified by its encroachment. One of the pervasive image patterns of the play is that of overpowering enclosure. Willy's fear of being swallowed up is dramatically pictured at the rise of the curtain.

> Before us is the Salesman's house. We are aware of towering, angular shapes behind it surrounding it on all sides. Only the blue light of the sky falls upon the house and the forestage; the surrounding area shows an angry glow of orange. As more light appears, we see a solid vault of apartments around a small, fragile-seeming home.

The "small, fragile-seeming home" certainly suggests Willy's ego, which is described as skeletal, "wholly or, in some places, partially transparent." It is not, in other words, a solid house. Willy may brag about "all the cement, the lumber, the reconstruction" he put into it and can claim "There ain't a crack to be found in it anymore," but in truth it is pitifully open to the crushing and "solid" apartment houses above it. The city, as represented by the apartment houses bathed in an angry orange, is kind of a jungle. Ben advises, "Get out of these cities, they're full of talk and time payments and courts of law." Willy should "screw on his fists" and leave. But Willy will never leave the city again. Since he is not able to "drive the car," he rages against the way he is being swallowed up by the city:

> Willy: Why don't you open a window in here, for God's sake?
>
> Linda, with infinite patience: They're all open, dear.
>
> Willy: The way they boxed us in here. Bricks and windows, windows and bricks.
>
> Linda: We should've bought the land next door.
>
> Willy: The street is lined with cars. There's not a breath of fresh air in the neighborhood. The grass don't grow any more, you can't raise

a carrot in the back yard. They should've
had a law against apartment houses.

The city and the jungle are opposite: one has trees, the other
is made of concrete; one is desirable and one is horrifying.
But the jungle and the city are really just Willy's different
perceptions of the same thing: the unconscious state he wishes
to return to.   The opposite forms represent his longing, on
the one hand, and the fear of what he longs for, on the other.
Paradoxically, the more his needs cause him to wish for trees,
the more completely he imagines himself to be surrounded by
concrete.

Of all the ways the mind has for formulating the inner need
to return to the womb, the symbol of sexual intercourse has
probably remained the most compelling.   It is easy to theorize
why.   The sexual act itself demands a certain loss of ego, a
certain giving away to the flood of instinctual emotions, and
after orgasm there is often a complete, if temporary, loss of
ego control.   Beyond this, of course, in a very physical sense
the womb is inside the female body and the way to it is through
its opening.   At first glance, however, it would seem unlikely
that Willy's need to return to the womb is expressed as a
desire for sexual intercourse.   He appears far too exhausted,
far too confused, far too consumed with other worries.   And his
feelings toward Linda simply do not appear to be sensual.
Nevertheless, I suggest that Willy's suicide can be best
imagined as a sexual act.   Miller certainly describes the
culmination of his suicide in terms strongly suggestive of an
orgasm:

> . . . . sounds, faces, voices, seem to be
> swarming in on him. . . . [The music] rises
> in intensity, almost to an unbearable
> scream. He goes up and down on his toes. . . .
> As the car speeds off, the music crashes down
> in a frenzy of sound, which becomes the soft
> pulsation of a single cello string.

If Willy views his suicide as an act of sexual intercourse,
toward whom are his sexual passions pointed?   One helpful key
is to ask for whom the suicide is intended.   At first, that
someone appears to be Linda.   Willy tells Ben, "'Cause she's
suffered, Ben, the woman has suffered."   The proposition is
"Terrific, terrific," because Linda will get the $20,000.   But
Willy quickly changes the focus, never to return to Linda.   The
rest of his motivation for the suicide centers on Biff.

> . . . that boy will be thunderstruck, Ben,
> because he never realized--I am known, Ben,
> and he'll see it with his eyes once and for

all. He'll see what I am, Ben! He's in for
a shock, that boy.

Willy wonders how he can get back to the good old times
with Biff and why he can't "give him something and not have
him hate me." And after his argument with Biff, and after Biff
cries on his shoulder, Willy can call out, "Oh, Biff! . . .
That boy--that boy is going to be magnificent!" Before, the
$20,000 may have been intended for Linda, but now it is intended
for Biff. Willy has Ben say, "Yes, outstanding, with twenty
thousand behind him" and to that Willy adds, "Can you imagine
that magnificence with twenty thousand dollars in his pocket?"
The suicide is to be more than a sacrifice for money. It is
to be an act of love. Willy has been tremendously moved that
Biff "cried to me." Willy is "almost dancing." He calls out,
"Oh, if I could kiss him, Ben!" Willy is astounded that Biff
"Loves me. Always loved me." Miller describes Willy as
"choking with love." He is sure that Biff will "worship me."
And he cries out in what is almost his last line in the play,
"Oh, Ben, I always knew one way or another we were gonna make
it, Biff and I!"

This explosion of emotion suggests, improbable as it may
seem, that Willy has a lover's feelings for the boy. Willy
certainly acts like a jealous lover. Linda tells Biff that

> When you write you're coming, he's all
> smiles, and talks about the future, and--
> he's just wonderful. And then the closer
> you seem to come, the more shaky he gets, and
> then by the time you get here, he's arguing,
> and he seems angry at you.

Willy criticizes Biff as soon as he gets off the train, he
worries whether Biff apologized to him, he wonders how Biff can
find himself on a farm, claims he's lazy, claims he's not lazy,
promises to get him a job selling, is terrified that he's
leaving, grows ecstatic when he hears about Biff's idea to
seek help from Oliver, grows critical when he finds a weakness
in the plan, and so on. As Happy says, Willy has been talking
more and more to himself lately, and "most of the time he's
talking to you [Biff]." The most explosive emotions in the
play are between Willy and Biff. Whenever they are brought
together, a confrontation follows. Their final, no-holds
barred argument, is the obligatory scene. The rest of the play
builds to that scene; to a large extent the play is about that
scene.

Of course, parents have strong feelings about their children, but why should Willy have developed such intense feelings
toward Biff? If a clinician were writing a quick sketch of

66

Willy's personality, one of the patterns he would point to is
the exaggerated awe in which Willy holds men of stature and
power. He wants to be like Dave Singleman, claims that Old
Man Wagner would have protected him, hangs on Ben's every word,
and desperately seeks his approval. On the other hand, he
needs to imagine he is the equal of these men, brags about
his business success, needs to be thought of as a "Big Shot,"
and in a hallucination can tell his sons,

> I never have to wait in line to see a buyer.
> "Willy Loman is here!" That's all they have
> to know, and I go right through.

We do not have to seek far to find the cause for this adolescent
attitude toward older men. There is some evidence that Willy's
father left the family while Willy was quite young, and Willy,
in a hallucination, is articulate about the effect of this
desertion:

> You're just what I need, Ben, because I--I
> have a fine position here, but I--well, Dad left
> when I was such a baby and I never had a chance
> to talk to him and I still feel--kind of temporary
> about myself.

Evidently Willy had no father to identify with and thus help
him find an identity as an adult male. Having been denied
this, he has continually looked for that approval from father
figures, men of stature and power, in his adult life.
Similarly, since he is not sure he is an adult male, he must
brag to everyone that he is tremendously successful in the
competitive, male-dominated business world.

Typically the man who is not sure he is an adult male is
terrified of adult women. While Willy's terror of women is
not apparent from the surface of the play (Linda seems such a
supportive wife), his constant fear of enclosure can also be
understood as a projection of his terror of being overwhelmed
by a woman. The towering apartment houses, lit by an angry
glow of orange, which surround and enclose the stage, appear
ready to crush his "small, fragile-seeming home." Without the
ability to drive his "car" Willy is trapped in the city and
projects on to the city an enclosing nature: it's boxed him
in, there are too many bricks, no air, no grass, carrots don't
grow, trees have disappeared and they've "massacred the neighborhood."

In his occupation Willy spends most of his time escaping
from the enclosure of the city by going on the road. And in
this sense he is adolescently promiscuous. He is like a man
who, because of his own fears, refuses to make love to a willing

wife, but has numerous quick affairs in which he hopes to make
a "conquest" and not be "trapped." He leaves the enclosure
of New York City to go to New England where he feels "vital,"
but in New England he goes into cities: Providence, Waterbury,
Boston, Portland, Bangor and so forth. And he likes to think
he has been successful. He brags he has no trouble getting
in: "'Willy Loman is here!' That's all they have to know,
and I go right through." Part of the reason for this success
is that his "car" is safe there: "the cops protect it like
their own." He even casts these successes in the sporting
and killing terminology that adolescent boys use when describing
their victories to their friends: "Knocked 'em cold in
Providence, slaughtered them in Boston." This sort of talk
implies an adversary role where the man not only enjoys the
woman, but kills her off so she is no longer around to terrify
him.

The imagery of the play suggests another quality about the
area into which Willy escapes. There is a "frontier" association to much of the area to which Willy is attracted. Willy's
father supposedly threw his family into a wagon and crossed
all the western states, Ben talks about a new continent at
Willy's doorstep, Willy longs for the timberland of Alaska,
he admires Ben for cracking the jungle, he refers to his sales
area as a territory (which, Willy implies, was so far north
the Wagner Company didn't even know it existed), and in a
hallucination he tries to convince Ben that Brooklyn is a sort
of wilderness:

> No, Ben, I don't want you to think. . . . It's
> Brooklyn, I know, but we hunt too. . . . Oh,
> sure, there's snakes and rabbits and—that's
> why I moved out here.

This "frontier" implies virgin territory. The implication is
that these new territories have not yet been touched by man
and are as yet unspoiled. This fantasy is again familiar in
the man who is terrified of the mature, experienced, available
woman: he is interested in virgins, opening up new territory,
cracking the jungle where no other man has been.

The frontier suggests the riches to be found in the heart
of these untouched territories. Both Alaska and Africa contain
precious metals. Hall points out that unconsciously men have
a "conception of the female genitals [as] a place where
valuables are stored" [1953, p. 169]. Willy can view his
father's flight to Alaska as a sexual venture. There were
"three gold strikes in one month in Alaska" and Willy felt like
going along, "Just for the ride, you might say." Similarly he
admires Ben's success in an exaggerated way. True, Ben has been
a successful businessman (there is objective evidence for this),

but it is not his business success that intrigues Willy. Willy
is attracted by the fact that he found riches in the jungle.
The dark jungle suggests the vagina and Ben is a man who has
successfully penetrated it and found diamonds.

All this helps us to understand why Willy has developed
such strong feelings for his son, Biff. Ovesey has developed
an interesting theory he calls "pseudo-homosexuality" [1955].
He argues that when a man feels he is not a complete man and
is therefore terrified of the consequences of sexual intercourse with women, he will wish to incorporate the power and
strength of an older more successful man. At the same time,
since such a desire is an admission that he is not a man, he
will attempt to deny this need by constantly trying to
demonstrate that he is more powerful than the stronger man.
He will at the same time, in other words, be both dependent
and combative.

We certainly see this mix of feelings in Willy's attitudes
toward Biff. On the one hand, he wants to be the son of his
own son. He attempts to build up in Biff all the qualities of
success that will make Biff strong. He has, Willy thinks, all
the magic potential. He is good looking, all the girls chase
after him, he is the star of the football team, three
universities are after him. In the future

> his name will sound out like a bell and all
> the doors will open to him.

On the other hand, he cannot stand the thought of success in
Biff (which would be tantamount to admitting his own dependency),
so he constantly criticizes Biff. In the first act when Willy
learns that Biff is going to see Oliver and become successful,
he is enthusiastic:

> There's fifty men in the City of New York
> who'd stake him.

> . . . .

> He knows something about it. You know
> sporting goods better than Spalding, for
> God's sake!

However, the defense against this excitement surfaces and he
begins to tear Biff down:

> Willy: How much is he giving you?

> Biff: I don't know, I didn't even see him
> yet, but--

Willy: Then what're you talkin' about?

Biff, getting angry: Well, all I said was I'm gonna see him, that's all!

Willy, turning away: Ah, you're counting your chickens again.

Biff, starting left for the stairs: Oh, Jesus, I'm going to sleep!

Willy, calling after him: Don't curse in this house!

Biff, turning: Since when did you get so clean?

Happy, trying to stop them: Wait a. . .

Willy: Don't use that language to me! I won't have it!

Similarly, Willy's first response to Biff's involvement in the water polo idea is enthusiastic:

That's an idea!

. . . .

That is a one-million-dollar idea!

. . . .

Lick the world! You guys together could absolutely lick the civilized world.

But almost immediately Willy attempts to control Biff and to show that he, Willy, has the superior knowledge. He instructs Biff to wear a sport jacket and slacks, to wear a business suit, walk in seriously, walk in with a big laugh, don't say "Gee," don't look worried, and so forth. Again and again he interrupts Linda:

Linda: He loved you.

Willy: Will you stop!

. . . .

Linda: Oliver always thought the highest of him——

70

Willy: Will you let me talk?

. . . .

Linda: Willy—

Willy: Don't take his side all the time,
goddammit.

In her enthusiasm she emphasizes how great Biff is going to be,
and Willy cannot bear this.

Willy's need to deny his dependency on Biff takes the form
of wishing Biff to be a failure. The proof of this unconscious wish can be found in the unusual guilt Willy feels
about Biff's lack of success. The dynamics are: since I want
Biff to be a failure, and since he is a failure, I am
responsible for his failure. In a moment of honesty he
comments to Bernard,

> Bernard, Bernard, was it my fault? Y'see?
> It keeps going around in my mind, maybe I
> did something to him.

Generally, however, he is not so honest. Rather he denies his
guilty feelings about Biff's failures by projecting his feelings on Biff. That is, Willy does not want to hurt Biff by
having Biff fail; instead, Biff wants to fail so he can hurt
Willy. The strongest example of this projection is at the
end of the play. Biff, who appears to be in a forgiving mood,
comes to Willy to tell him that he has decided to go back out
West and he emphasizes, "To hell with whose fault it is or
anything like that." Willy, however, is "frozen, immobile,
with guilt in his voice. . . . " Biff again emphasizes, "This
isn't your fault; it's me, I'm a bum." And he wants to shake
hands and clear things up: "You gonna wish me luck, scout? He
extends his hand. What do you say?" But Willy is unable to
accept forgiveness. He turns to Linda: "Spite, see?" And to
Biff:

> Spite, spite, is the word of your undoing!
> And when you're down and out, remember what
> did it. When you're rotting somewhere beside
> the railroad tracks, remember, and don't you
> dare blame it on me!

Biff repeats he is not blaming Willy, but Willy exclaims, "I
won't take the rap for this, you hear?" Angered, Biff reveals
the ultimate in his failure. He has been a petty criminal: "I
stole a suit in Kansas City and I was in jail." Willy's
response is typical: "I suppose that's my fault!"

Not only in "real life" does Willy have a need for Biff to fail, but in his hallucinations as well. Again, we must remember that these hallucinations are to be understood as dreams, as expressions of hidden wishes. Schneider points out that in the play,

> The past, as in hallucination, comes back to him [Willy], not chronologically as in a "flashback," but dynamically with the inner logic of his erupting volcanic unconscious [1949, p. 18. Emphasis in text.]

What is notable in these hallucinations is how often Biff fails. True, the first hallucination begins with Biff at the peak of his potential: the budding young athlete and future Big Man On Campus. He can steal a football and get away with it. He is not nervous about the upcoming game, and the girls follow him around after class. But the same hallucination ends on quite another note. Biff is in trouble. Bernard asks, "Where is he? If he doesn't study!" Linda nags, "And he'd better give back that football, Willy, it's not nice." Linda claims that Biff is too rough with the girls and that "All the mothers are afraid of him." Bernard adds that "He's driving the car without a license!" and that "Mr. Birnbaum says he's stuck up," and that he will probably "flunk math!" At the same time we hear the mocking laugh of the woman in Boston. In this hallucination Willy may attempt to deny the wish to have Biff fail ("There's nothing the matter with him!"), but it is, after all, Willy's hallucination and he is responsible for the material in it.

Similarly, the second hallucination in the first act is notable for all the material it contains concerning Biff's failure. Ben asks Biff to engage him in a practice fight, and before Biff knows what has happened to him he has been tripped up and defeated by Ben. Biff's reaction is that of a boy, not a successful man: "Gee!" Although Willy sends Biff and Happy out on a stealing mission, it ends in failure. Charlie suggests that "if they steal any more from that building the watchman'll put the cops on them," and that Biff may very well end up in jail. Bernard rushes in to exclaim, "The watchman's chasing Biff." And Linda, who is alarmed, leaves to find Biff. Again, Willy may attempt to deny the possibility of Biff's failure ("There's nothing wrong. What's the matter with you?"), but, again, he is responsible for the material in the hallucination.

Finally, and most importantly, we should understand that Willy's desperate need to gain strength from Biff takes a sexual form. In his theory of "pseudo-homosexuality" Ovesey postulates that the desire to gain the older man's power is expressed through the unconscious fantasy of incorporating orally or anally the symbol of that other man's masculinity: his penis. He will want the stronger man to have intercourse with him either in the mouth or the anus. Ovesey records the history of a patient who developed the following masturbatory technique to gain the power of his father so that he might have intercourse with his mother:

> He manipulated his penis with one hand while he pumped a thermometer in and out of his anus with the other. In the fantasy that accompanied this act, he imagined himself sandwiched between his mother and his father as they were having intercourse. The father's penis entered the patient's anus, emerged as the patient's penis, and then penetrated the mother's vagina. . . . The patient. . . incorporated the father's penis and magically made use of its strength to repair his own weakness. . . [1955, p. 396].

Ovesey points out that this patient incorporated his father's penis in fantasy not only in sexual situations, but in non-sexual situations that called for assertion and which therefore generated severe anxiety. At such times "He would retire to the nearest lavatory, give his anus a few quick strokes with a thermometer, and then go out and try and assert himself" [ibid., p. 397]. Ovesey records that another patient had a history of being scoffed at by his wife because he was "not a man."

> That same night he dreamed that he went to a butcher shop and ate several hunks of meat. He identified the butcher as the therapist [the stronger male]. Then he spontaneously associated "penis" to the meat, and suggested that it was up to the therapist to provide what he lacked. Thus the dream had satisfied this demand through a fellatio fantasy in which he orally incorporated the therapist's penis. Equipped in this way, he felt that he could magically go ahead, resolve his inhibition of aggression. . . and so stand up as a man to his wife [ibid., p. 396. My emphasis].

Since Willy feels inadequate as a man and is terrified of women, he desperately needs Biff to overpower and penetrate him.

One of the memories Willy returns to again and again is the incident in the hotel room in Boston. Without question, something dramatic happened there. But the scene as Willy remembers it is not necessarily an accurate reproduction of what

actually happened. His memories of Boston are, we must
remember, hallucinated material, just as are his memories of
the "old days" and the scenes with Ben. Therefore the Boston
incident--at least the evidence about it given to us in the
play--must be considered as a dream, as a symbolic event. We
must go beyond its manifest content.

Willy appears to hallucinate about the Boston incident
whenever he feels particularly strongly that he is a failure
and is unable to get strength from Biff to compensate for that
sense of failure. The most obvious example is in the second
act after he has suffered the humiliation of being fired by
Howard. He goes to the Chop House hoping to hear good news of
Biff's business success. But instead, Biff insists on holding
"on to the facts tonight, Pop. We're not going to get anywhere
bullin' around." As Biff proceeds to relate his adventures with
Oliver, and more than that, tries to demonstrate to Willy
that he, Biff, is not a successful type of person, Willy's
mind drifts off until he is no longer listening to Biff but is
totally absorbed in his hallucination of the Boston incident.

For whatever reason, then, there appears to be a connection
between Willy's powerful sense of inadequacy, Biff's failure to
support him by being big himself, and his hallucinations of
Boston. What is that connection?

As with most dreams, there is a contradiction within the
manifest content of the Boston incident. The woman in the
hotel room gives him two opposite sorts of advice. On the
one hand, she nags him to open the door ("Aren't you going to
answer the door? He'll wake the whole hotel"). On the other
hand, she nags him to forget the door ("Come on inside, drummer
boy. It's silly to be dressing in the middle of the night").
In asking him to ignore the door and "come on inside" she is
asking him to go to bed with her. The "Raw sensuous music"
that accompanies her speech, the fact that it is a hotel room,
her insistence that he have another drink, her flattery of him,
and her confidence that Willy will "go right through" in the
future all suggest the same desire on her part. Her insistence
that Willy open the door to stop the knocking does not have to
be a contradiction. Indeed, it can be seen as another way of
expressing the same desires. Since we are dealing with the
incident as a dream, the woman herself may be symbolized as a
hotel room with a door that can be (and, indeed, which she
wishes to be) opened: she says, "I felt the knocking." Thus
when she says, "Aren't you going to answer the door?" she is
suggesting that he open her door. Looked at in this way, the
following lines of hers offer no contradiction:

> Come on inside drummer boy. It's silly to
> be dressing in the middle of the night. As

knocking is heard: Aren't you going to answer
the door?

In answering and opening the "door," Willy will "Come on inside."

This hallucination suggests how Willy attempts to defend
against being enveloped and swallowed during sexual intercourse.
On the simplest level he attempts to escape from the woman's
bedroom by having someone knocking on the door so he can dress
and project his anxiety on the knocking, the clerk at the desk,
the possibility of fire, and so forth, rather than suffer the
consequences of staying with the woman. On a deeper level it
is significant too that Biff is the one who is knocking, trying
to get in. The hotel room may also be understood, not as the
woman, but as Willy; the door not as the woman's orifice, but
as Willy's. Therefore, the dream suggests that as Willy is
under pressure to enter the woman, he needs Biff to enter him.
Since he feels inadequate to satisfy the woman, he wants Biff
to penetrate him, so he will, via incorporation, be potent
enough to enter the woman.

We are now in a better position to understand why Willy
slips into this hallucination when he does. He has just been
unmanned, made impotent, by Howard. This, as the hallucination
shows, leaves him terribly vulnerable to women. He needs
strength desperately from a stronger, more successful male. He
attempts to gain that strength from Biff in the Chop House:
"Well, what happened, boy? Nodding affirmatively, with a smile.
Everything go all right?" But when Biff starts to suggest that
everything did not go all right ("Dad, I don't know who said it
first, but I was never a salesman for Bill Oliver"), Willy cuts
him short:

> I'm not interested in stories about the past
> or any crap of that kind because the woods are
> burning, boys, you understand? There's a big
> blaze going on all around. I was fired today.

In other words, Biff must pretend to be successful so that Willy
has "a little good news to tell your mother." But Biff has no
good news. At this point Willy goes into his hallucination of
the Boston incident, which is, as we have seen, primarily a
hidden wish that Biff enter him so that he may have the potency
to enter a woman.

However, Willy does not succeed in his hallucination in
getting Biff to enter him. Biff never gets in the room but
rather tells Willy, "Dad--I let you down." Biff goes away
calling Willy a phony, a fake. It is not surprising that after
Willy, in "real life," comes out of the bathroom in the
restaurant (where he has experienced the bulk of the hallucina-

tion) his thoughts turn, albeit in a pathetic way, to re-establishing his masculinity. He asks Stanley, the waiter, "Tell me--is there a seed store in the neighborhood?" Willy explains,

> Oh, I'd better hurry. I've got to get some
> seeds. I've got to get some seeds, right
> away. Nothing's planted. I don't have a
> thing in the ground.

Returning home, Willy goes outside, at night, to plant seeds: "Carrots. . . quarter-inch apart. Rows. . . one-foot rows."

Just as his last hallucination centered on a sexual in-volvement with a woman, his hallucination as he plants seeds concerns the act of suicide, which, represents the act of sexual intercourse, as a way of returning to the womb. The attempt to plant seeds is an attempt to assure himself he will not be swallowed up by death. He tries to convince himself that by entering Africa he will give Linda something. She will get the insurance money. Because, as he tells Ben, "a man has got to add up to something." A man has to have a penis. "A man can't go out the way he came in, Ben. . . ." In this context "out" really means "in." A man may originally come out of the womb without much of a penis, but when he goes back in, he had better have one. He wants Ben to "go through the ins and outs of the thing with me. . . ." And Willy is encouraged by the thought that "twenty-thousand--that is something one can feel with the hand," [Emphasis in text]. Surely what he wants to feel in his hand is his penis. Willy fantacizes that his funeral will be "massive." Biff may think "I'm nothing, see," but Biff will "see it with his eyes once and for all."

But this whole attempt to convince himself that he is "massive" collapses when Biff comes out into the back yard. The images of threatening enclosure once again float into consciousness: "You can't see nothing out here! They boxed in the whole goddam neighborhood!" Biff has come to tell Willy that he, Biff, is a failure, that he will not see Oliver, that he is leaving and is never coming back. When Biff suggests they go inside to tell the news to Linda, Willy stands "frozen, immobile." Without the possibility of strength from Biff "I don't want to see her." But Biff forces him inside, and once there Willy develops a new strategy to demonstrate how Biff's departure is actually an attempt on Biff's part to give him strength: "with full accusation: You're trying to put a knife in me--don't think I don't know what you're doing!" This, of course, flies in the face of what Biff is saying: that he's not phallically oriented, that he's a dollar an hour, that he's someone who "couldn't raise it," that he's not bringing home any more prizes, that "I'm nothing!"

76

But something else is happening in the scene that is very
gratifying to Willy. As the scene progresses, Biff gets more
and more explosively angry at Willy. Soon, even though Biff
is saying that he is not phallic, he demonstrates a real fury,
a real rage in his attack. Biff is on the verge of actually,
physically, assaulting his father. At the height of the argument, "<u>Biff starts for Willy, but is blocked by Happy. In his
fury, Biff seems on the verge of attacking his father</u>." But
Happy cannot restrain Biff. "<u>Biff breaks from Happy. Willy, in
fright, starts up the stairs. Biff grabs him</u>." Oddly enough,
this very assault is coupled with evidence that Biff loves Willy,
for as his fury peaks he breaks down and cries in his father's
arms. The result is clear: Willy is elated. Primarily, Willy's
elation stems from his perception that Biff's physical attack
was an attempt to overpower him sexually, an attempt for which
Willy had so desperately longed; secondarily, his elation
derives from Biff's show of love. Now that Biff has man-
handled Willy, Willy "<u>cries out his promise</u>," that boy is going
to be magnificent," and can have Ben say, "Yes, <u>outstanding</u> with
twenty-thousand behind him." To this Ben can add, "And it does
take a <u>great</u> kind of man to crack the jungle." The logic between
the sequence of these thoughts is: now that Biff has overpowered and loved me, he has shown me he is "out-standing," and
therefore I have the strength to go into the womb of death, into
the jungle.[3] Willy thinks of that "magnificence with twenty-
thousand dollars in his [Biff's] <u>pocket</u>." Because of this, "Oh
if I could kiss him, Ben!" Now the sexual meaning of the
following line is much clearer: "Oh, Ben, I always knew one
way or another we were gonna <u>make it</u>, Biff and I." Finally,
there is Willy's incantation to Biff (in fact, his last words in
the play) just as he is about to commit suicide and enter the
jungle, the womb. He uses football imagery, but he is asking
Biff for a <u>long</u> boot, to get low, and come in <u>under</u> the <u>ball</u>:

> <u>elegiacally, turning to the house</u>: Now when
> you kick off, boy, I want a seventy-yard boot,
> and get right down the field under the ball,
> and when you hit, hit low and hit hard, because
> it's important, boy.

Chapter IV

HAPPY

I

Linda, Biff and Willy at least seem to wish to be able to
reach out beyond themselves, to care about other human beings.
In contrast, Happy appears closed within himself. Since the
focus of his attention is always on his car, his women and his
apartment, we size him up as selfish, egocentric and insensitive.
He seems to be a lesser character, not worthy of our real
attention; this judgment is reflected in the lack of critical
comment on him.

One could argue, however, that Happy does reach out beyond
himself. In particular, Happy seems more concerned about Willy's
suffering than does Biff. At the beginning of the play, the
boys have been asleep when Willy comes back unexpectedly from
his trip. They awake and listen to Willy's ramblings. Biff
not only expresses no concern for Willy, but tries to avoid the
issue of Willy's desperation. It is Happy who appears anxious.
He has been waiting

> to talk to you about Dad for a long time,
> Biff. Something's happening to him. He
> talks to himself.

Happy worries that Willy may have smashed the car, that he may
have his license taken away, that he "doesn't seem to keep his
mind on it [his driving]." Biff tries to dismiss this concern
by ascribing Willy's difficulties to old age ("His eyes are
going"), but Happy will not be put off. Happy understands that
a good part of what is bothering Willy has to do with Willy's
feelings about Biff: "Most of the time he's talking about you."
Although Biff tries to avoid the subject, Happy suggests that
Biff's behavior is causing some of Willy's problems:

> I think the fact that you're not settled,
> that you're still kind of up in the air.

79

Happy tells Biff what he must do to help Willy:

> You'll find a job here. You gotta stick
> around. I don't know what to do about him,
> it's getting embarrassing.

Given this concern, it is not surprising that Happy, not Biff,
finally goes downstairs and tries to get Willy to go off to bed;
Happy is still trying when Charlie comes over and signals Happy
that he will attempt to put Willy to bed.

However, Willy won't go to bed and wanders out into the
garden. No one can sleep. Linda and Biff get in a long discussion, and at the end of this discussion Biff promises to
apply himself. But when Willy comes back into the house from
the garden, an argument flares up immediately between him and
Biff. Willy starts to walk out of the room and Biff threatens
to leave town the next day. Happy figures a way out of the
crisis: "He's going to see Bill Oliver, Pop." Willy becomes
enthusiastic, and the crisis is eased. As always, however,
father and son start arguing again:

> Biff: Oh, Jesus, I'm going to sleep.
>
> Willy: Don't curse in this house.
>
> Biff: Since when did you get so clean?

Again, Happy stops the argument:

> Wait a minute! I got an idea. I got a
> feasible idea. Come here, Biff, let's talk
> this over now, let's talk some sense here.

He proposes his water polo idea. Willy is delighted and again
the crisis is defused. Yet, again, before long Biff and Willy
are arguing and, furious, Willy goes off to bed. Linda suggests
that Biff go up and say good night, and Happy picks up the idea:
"Come on Biff, let's buck him up." When for the first time in
the play Biff seems to express some confidence and talks about
buying a new tie so he can make an impression on Oliver, Happy
immediately understands that this would be good for Willy.

> Come on up. Tell that to Dad. Let's give
> him a whirl.

When they arrive upstairs, Happy generously leaves himself out
of the discussion: "He [Biff] wanted to say good night to you,
sport."

In the second act, the first time Biff and Willy are

together, a collision seems imminent. Biff has been humiliated
at Oliver's and wants to tell the truth to Willy regardless
of the consequences. Willy has been fired and desperately needs
to hear that Biff is a success. When Happy meets Biff in the
Chop House and understands what his brother is going to tell
Willy, Happy objects: "You crazy? What for?" Biff says that
Willy has to know that he, Biff, is not the kind of man who
can be a success. But Happy counters, "You tell him something
nice," and thinks up a scheme:

> You leave the house tomorrow and come back
> at night and say Oliver is thinking it over
> for a couple of weeks; and gradually it fades
> away and nobody's the worse.

Nevertheless, when Willy enters, Biff tries to get the story
out, and Willy attempts to demand good news from Biff by
announcing that he, himself, has just been fired. Throughout
the ensuing argument, Happy attempts to help Willy by inter-
preting everything concerning Biff as "good news":

> Willy [to Biff]: You mean you didn't go up
> there [to Oliver's]?
>
> Happy: Sure he went up there.
>
> . . . .
>
> Willy: So tell me, he gave you a warm welcome?
>
> Happy: Sure, Pop, sure!
>
> . . . .
>
> Willy: Imagine, a man doesn't see him for ten,
> twelve years and gives him that kind of welcome!
>
> Happy: Damn right!
>
> . . . .
>
> Willy: Very hard man to see, y'know.
>
> Happy: Oh, I know.
>
> . . . .
>
> Biff: Yeah, he gave me a couple of--no, no!
>
> Happy: He told him my Florida idea.

When Biff tries to tell the truth, Happy stops him:

> Biff: I waited six hours—
>
> Happy: What the hell are you saying?

And when Biff manages to convince Willy that he actually stole
Oliver's pen, Happy is ready with an excuse so that Willy will
not be hurt:

> He just had it in his hand when Oliver walked
> in so he got nervous and stuck it in his pocket!

As Willy gets more and more desperate in the face of Biff's
revelations, Happy comforts him:

> He'll strike something, Pop.
>
> . . . .
>
> He's gonna be terrific, Pop!

When Biff and Willy almost get into a physical fight, _Happy_
attempts to separate them.

At the end of the second act, during the most intense
argument between Biff and Willy, Happy once again acts as a
peacemaker. Having already retired upstairs, he comes down
and watches. Again, as always, he moves to keep the confrontation from becoming full-blown. When Biff, calling Willy a
phony, pulls out the rubber hose and puts it on the table,
Happy's reaction is, "You crazy—" At the height of the argument when the stage directions tell us that "Biff seems on the
verge of attacking his father," and, he, in fact, starts for
Willy, he "is blocked by Happy." When, instead of attacking
Willy, Biff breaks down and sobs in his father's arms, Happy
is deeply moved:

> Willy: Isn't that—isn't that remarkable?
> Biff—he likes me!
>
> Linda: He loves you Willy.
>
> Happy, _deeply moved_: Always did, Pop.

Happy's remarks in the Requiem are a continuation of his
support for Willy. Biff attacks Willy because "He had the
wrong dreams." Happy cannot stand for this: "almost ready to
fight Biff: Don't say that!" And when Biff tells Charlie "the
man never knew who he was," Happy again objects: "infuriated:
Don't say that!" In fact, Happy will prove that

Willy Loman did not die in vain. He had a
good dream. It's a good dream. It's the
only dream you can have--to come out number
one man. He fought it out here, and this
is where I'm gonna win it for him.

II

What I have presented above is the case that could be made
to demonstrate that Happy cares deeply about Willy's welfare.
Enough evidence supports this contention so that it cannot be
completely disregarded.

Yet it is also easy to make a case that Happy cares nothing
for Willy and isn't concerned whether he lives or dies. Willy's
emotional troubles have been coming on for some time. Other
than sending Willy to Florida and giving him fifty dollars last
Christmas, Happy has done nothing for Willy. Linda points out
that Happy is hardly ever around the house:

Happy: I never heard him so loud, Mom.

Linda: Well, come around more often, you'll
hear him.

Happy doesn't really start to be concerned about Willy until
Biff comes home (a point to which I will return later).

Yet even during the course of the play--after Biff's
arrival--Happy's attitude toward Willy is often callous. We
see this attitude at its extreme in the Chop House scene. The
boys, we should remember, are throwing the dinner for Willy's
benefit. Linda is pleased about the meal because "you'll save
his life." The purpose of the dinner is for Willy to celebrate
Biff's getting a good job. Happy arrives first at the restaurant.
We would expect to find him concerned about two things: how
Willy will enjoy the meal, and whether Biff got the job. In
fact, Happy's attention is focused in another direction. A
girl walks in and Happy tries to pick her up. In contrast, when
Biff comes in he is interested in Willy: "Is Dad here?" Happy
doesn't care and tries to involve Biff in picking up the girl:

Biff: Isn't Dad coming?

Happy: You want her?

Biff refuses to get involved and attempts to bring up a subject

which will have important ramifications when Willy arrives: his
success with Oliver. But Happy disregards this topic and again
tries to involve Biff with the girl:

> Wait a minute. I've got to see that old
> confidence again. Do you want her? She's
> on call.

Then Happy does something which cannot in any way be reconciled
with the notion that he cares for Willy's well-being. He asks
the girl to get a friend:

> Happy: Honey? Are you busy?

> Girl: Well I am. . . but I could make a phone
> call.

> Happy: Do that, will you honey? And see if
> you can get a friend. We'll be here for a while.

Happy is setting up a night on the town for Biff. He seems
unaware that Willy will be arriving momentarily.

Still, when Biff finally forces Happy's attention to his
lack of success with Oliver, Happy counsels him to lie to Willy;
when Willy arrives Happy attempts to make it appear that Biff
has been successful; and Happy tries to stop an incipient fight
between them. However, whatever concern he shows toward Willy
evaporates when the girls arrive:

> Well girls, what's the program? We're wasting
> time. Come on, Biff. Gather round. Where
> would you like to go?

When Biff runs out, Happy, instead of staying with his father,
who is in the bathroom, chooses to follow Biff. When one of
the girls asks Happy if he doesn't want to say goodbye to his
father, Happy can say, "No that's not my father. He's just a
guy." As Linda will say later,

> Not one, not another living soul would have
> had the cruelty to walk out on that man in
> a restaurant.

Of course, anyone can make a mistake. At least Happy's
selfish behavior might be excused if he later realized the
gravity of his actions and asked forgiveness. But the reverse
is true. He tries to defend what he did as correct. When the
two boys return home to a waiting Linda, Happy explains that
the reason for leaving Willy was that "We met two girls, Mom,
very fine types," and that nothing was wrong because Willy "had

a swell time with us." Certainly, he tells Linda, he didn't abandon Willy:

> Listen, when I—desert him I hope I don't
> outlive the day.

In one sense, even Happy's refusal to ask forgiveness could be defended if he really were unaware—as he claims—that he did anything wrong. But this simply is not true. The boys try to <u>sneak</u> <u>in</u>. Happy, who is in the lead, gives the OK sign to Biff only <u>after</u> he has determined that Linda is nowhere in sight. And Happy carries roses which, of course, are intended to mollify Linda. But when Linda makes her presence known and walks toward Happy, he "<u>backs</u> <u>up</u> <u>into</u> <u>the</u> <u>kitchen,</u> <u>afraid.</u>"

III

Happy's behavior, then, presents something of a paradox. Happy is a selfish, insouciant person without much inclination to care about anyone other than himself. In particular, he has done almost nothing for his father before the opening of the play, and at a crucial moment during the play leaves him "babbling in the toilet." Yet, oddly enough, Happy is also very much aware of what is happening to his father, cares for him, and does any number of things to protect and help him.

Happy, perhaps partly due to his name, fails to engage our empathy since he doesn't seem to have the capacity (as Biff and Willy and Linda so obviously have) for human suffering. He may be selfish, but he is, well, "happy." His sort always gets along one way or another. However, I suggest that Happy suffers intensely, that he has deep and searing problems. Happy may hide all this from himself and others, but he suffers great emotional pain and is desperately trying to find relief from this pain. His helping Willy <u>and</u> his ignoring Willy are a function of his desperation to escape that pain.

The clue which helps us understand his actions is that he only begins to attempt to help Willy (with a few exceptions noted above) when Biff comes home. Somehow Biff constitutes an important link in Happy's fight to relieve his pain. I suggest that Happy urgently looks to Biff for help, love, support and strength; that Happy has made an unconscious identification with Willy; and that, therefore, one way Happy can get help, love, support and strength from Biff—albeit symbolically—is to get Biff to give help, love, support, and strength to Willy.

Happy's feeling toward men somewhat older than himself is, to say the least, ambivalent. On the one hand, he admires, indeed, almost idealizes the merchandise manager. He talks about how the "waves part in front of him" because "that's fifty-two thousand dollars a year coming through the revolving door. . . ." Happy admires the fact that the merchandise manager "just built a terrific estate on Long Island." Also, Happy wants to be like him. He claims that the merchandise manager is "a good friend of mine," and he hopes "to walk into the store the way he walks in." He needs to show him "that Hap Loman can make the grade." Happy implies that he is the assistant to the merchandise manager (which would explain the claim that the two of them are friends) because he tells Biff he can't be advanced until the merchandise manager dies. But, in fact, this claim is not true. At the end of the play Biff charges that Happy is one of the two assistants to the assistant.

> Happy: Well, I'm practically--
>
> Biff: You're practically full of it!

Happy has a low-level position with a low-level salary. The merchandise manager probably does not know who Happy is. Happy, unlike most people, does not talk about what must be his real relationships with his immediate co-workers and bosses, nor does he talk about his realistic chances for advancement to the next grade. Rather he finds it necessary to fantasize a relationship across an impossible gulf and advancement to an impossible position.

Therefore we are not surprised to discover that Happy also harbors an enormous anger at the merchandise manager and others in his position whom he wishes to emulate. He feels he's

> got more in my pinky finger than he's [the merchandise manager's] got in his head.

Happy's going to "show some of those pompous, self-important executives" that he can succeed. More graphically, he wants to

> rip my clothes off in the middle of the store and outbox that goddam merchandise manager. I mean I can outbox, outrun, and outlift anybody in that store, and I have to take orders from those common, petty sons-of-bitches til I can't stand it anymore.

Even his motivation for going to bed with girls contains a hostile and competitive component toward his bosses. The very girl he was with this night and has "ruined", is engaged--so

86

Happy claims--to the man who will soon be vice-president of the store. Furthermore, he claims that is the "third executive I've done that to." Happy admits that such actions are "crummy" but puts it down to "an overdeveloped sense of competition."

This intense and ambivalent attitude toward the merchandise manager and other high-level executives at the store can be explained if we understand that these men are associated in Happy's mind with Biff. If we can trust information from Willy's hallucinations, Happy, as a child, always lived in the shadow of his more successful older brother. Biff was the good looking, all-American high school hero. He was captain of the football team; girls followed him around between classes. More important, Willy doted on and favored Biff. In the previous chapter I demonstrated how jealous Happy was of Biff and how he fought Biff for his father's attention and affection. Happy has evidently grown up with an exaggerated sense of envy and hostility toward Biff. It has become his goal in life to become like Biff, to attain Biff's high and favored position; yet, since that gulf is so wide, since Biff is so impossibly above him, Happy harbors tremendous hostility toward Biff and wishes to defeat him. This theory would explain why Happy does not concern himself with those of more or less his own rank at the store. These people are too much like him. Rather he must fantasize about those impossibly above him.

Significantly, Happy's problems with authority figures are very similar to Willy's. In my chapter on Willy I demonstrate that Willy, also, has exaggerated feelings regarding men who have been successful in business; he both wants to be liked by them and is hostile to them. Happy and Willy share another characteristic: both are younger siblings of brothers they view as highly successful. The authority figures in Willy's life stand for his older brother, Ben. Willy has substituted Biff for Ben, and now responds to his son, Biff, as if Biff were his older brother, Ben. Therefore, Happy and Willy share another important characteristic: both envy and hate Biff.

IV

In my chapter on Willy I explore the strong passive component in his behavior. In brief, I argue that since Willy feels weak and inadequate as a man, he needs the strength of the older male, and that this need is fantasized as incorporating the stronger man's penis. One of Willy's strongest desires is to absorb Biff's superior strength, and this desire, finally, is fantasized

as having sexual intercourse with Biff. If Happy and Willy
share other characteristics, do they share this one as well?
Does Happy, that is, direct his sexual desires toward Biff?

Certainly Happy's excessive sexual life makes us wonder if
it is not motivated defensively. Often a man who compulsively
goes to bed with girl after girl is defending against his own
urgent need to be a "girl." The fantasy is: I wish to be
overpowered by a man; I can't admit this wish to myself; therefore, if I am successful in my sexual conquest of girls, I
don't have a wish to be overpowered by a man. That Happy's
sexual life is defensive is further suggested by his interest
in women who will soon become the wives of high executives.
Such an interest indicates, on the one hand, a way of being like
the executives (i.e., I have the woman they have); on the other
hand, it can also express an identification with women who
will soon go to bed with the stronger male. The fantasy is:
this strong man is interested in this girl; I am intimate with
her; therefore he will be intimate with me. Such an identification is further suggested in a confusing speech Happy makes
about accepting bribes--a speech which, we should note, is a
continuation of and, according to Happy, an explanation of his
remarks about going to bed with fiances of high executives:

> Isn't that a crummy characteristic? And to
> top it all, I go to their weddings! Indignantly,
> but laughing: Like I'm not supposed to take
> bribes. Manufacturers offer me a hundred-dollar
> bill now and then to throw an order their way.
> You know how honest I am, but it's like this
> girl, see. I hate myself for it. Because I
> don't want the girl, and, still, I take it and--
> I love it.

On the surface Happy is saying that there are two sorts of
experiences he both hates and loves: going to bed with fiances
of high executives and taking bribes from manufacturers. He
manages to confuse the two experiences. Although he might
have said, "I take her and--I love it!", what he does say is, "I
take it and--I love it!" While "it" may certainly refer to the
act of taking the girl, "it" may also refer to the act of
taking bribes. Earlier he refers to that act as an "it": "It's
[taking bribes] like the girl, see." The act of taking a bribe
is a passive one. In a sense the manufacturer who offers him
one is treating him as a whore, asking him to "throw an order
their way." Happy tells Biff how "honest" he is, a term which
can also be applied to girls. But, as he says, "like this
girl" he takes the bribe, allows his honesty to be corrupted,
and hates it, yet loves it.

Another indication of Happy's passive nature occurs during

Willy's first hallucination. In the chapter on Biff, I discuss
the competition between the two boys for Willy's love. It is
clear that Biff is the more favored of the two. Willy announces
that he has a surprise for the boys which turns out to be a
punching bag. In response, Happy

> lies down on his back and pedals with his
> feet: I'm losing weight, you notice, Pop?

Happy attempts to get his father's attention by trying to show
that he is becoming as fit and as trim as Biff. Yet his
method of demonstrating this suggests a sexual passivity: he
has thrown his rear end up in the air as if it is this act he
wants his father to notice. Willy's response is curious as
well. "Jumping rope is good too." Jumping rope is good for
athletes. But in our society jumping rope is more often something girls do.

I argue in my chapter on Willy that it was very important
for Willy to regard Biff as a powerful and successful man--the
kind of man, in other words, one could get strength from; Happy,
too, must build up his image of Biff. In the first scene
between Happy and Biff, Happy's bringing up the subject of old
girl friends may seem gratuitous, but it is in part an attempt
to recall a time when Biff was the more powerful and successful
of the two. Happy pats his bed affectionately and suggests
that about "five hundred women" would have had an interest in
their conversations. But he points out that Biff was the
leader:

> You taught me everything I know about women.
> Don't forget that.

In a long rambling speech Biff recounts his attempts to hang
on to a series of low-level jobs out West and concludes that
"all I've done is to waste my life." Happy does not wish to
accept this conclusion, so rather than deal with what Biff has
said, he builds Biff up with compliments. He is not a failure:

> You're a poet, you know that Biff? You're
> a--you're an idealist.

An "idealist" is someone Happy looks up to as he reveals when
he tells Biff,

> everybody around me is so false that I'm
> constantly lowering my ideals. . . .

But Biff insists that he is a failure, that he's "mixed up very
bad," that he's "like a boy." Then he asks Happy if he, in
contrast, is successful. "You're a success aren't you. . . .

You're making money aren't you?" Again, especially considering Happy's need to lie about his rapid rise in the business world, we would expect him to brag about his many successes. And to a degree, as we have seen, he does. However, basically he refuses to place himself above Biff. Happy may appear to be a success, but actually he is a failure. True, he emulates the merchandise manager, but the merchandise manager is not happy. He built an estate in Long Island, but doesn't have the peace of mind to live in it. And, similarly, Happy has an apartment and a car, but can't enjoy them either. "I don't know what the hell I'm working for." He calls his condition "crazy" and admits, "And still, goddammit, I'm lonely." What is interesting about all this is that Happy encourages Biff to go into business to "find a job here." Yet he can tear down business as it relates to himself. The implication is that whereas business has not been fruitful for Happy, it will be for Biff.

V

Strangely enough, however, when Biff does decide (after a browbeating by Linda) to stay at home, get a job, and enter the business world, Happy gets upset. Before, Happy was of the opinion that Biff was well liked in the business world, but now he can claim,

> The trouble with you in business was you
> never tried to please people.

He criticizes Biff for doing "some damn fool thing like whistling whole songs in the elevator. . . ." Happy implies that Biff will never really make it in the business world since

> You don't raise a guy to a responsible job
> who whistles in the elevator. . . .

Concerning Biff's whistling in the elevator and swimming in the middle of the day, Happy must level with Biff:

> I'll tell you something that I hate to say,
> Biff, but in the business world some of them
> think you're crazy.

We can account for this seemingly paradoxical behavior if we see it as a function of Happy's strong passive sexual needs in relation to Biff. In my chapter on Willy I argue that just

90

as the weaker man wishes to gain the stronger man's strength
through the incorporation of that man's penis, he is ashamed
of and afraid of that act of sexual intercourse since that act
makes him appear passive and a "woman." Thus the man who feels
he is inadequate and wants the other man to be stronger will
at the same time, if the other man really is stronger, panic
and wish to fight him.

We see this reaction when, in the first scene between the
boys, Biff offers to take Happy out West with him. Biff's
idea is that they would buy a ranch, work in the open, and
share a life together. At first, as we would expect, Happy
is excited, even elated: "You and I, heh? . . . avidly: The
Loman Brothers, heh?" But the elation is quickly combined with
combativeness:

> enthralled: That's [going out West] what I
> dream about, Biff. Sometimes I want to just
> rip my clothes off in the middle of the store
> and outbox that goddam merchandise manager.
> I mean I can outbox, outrun, and outlift any-
> body in that store. . . .

Much as Happy tells Biff he wants to go, he first has to prove
to those "pompous, self-important executives that Hap Loman
can make the grade." After he has done that, "Then I'll go
with you, Biff." The merchandise manager and the other
executives at the store blend with Biff in Happy's mind. It is
not the executives Happy wishes to fight, but Biff. Biff,
in suggesting that Happy share an intimate experience with him
(going out West), feeds Happy's fears that he would be made
passive. Therefore, he must fantasize defeating Biff in combat
first. Only after Happy has assured himself that he can "make
the grade" and "outbox the others" can he feel easy about an
intimate relationship with Biff.

This panic also operates when it appears that Biff may be
successful in getting money from Oliver. At first, Happy is
elated:

> Come here, Biff, let's talk this over now,
> let's talk some sense here. . . . We form
> two basketball teams, see? Two water-polo
> teams. We play each other. . . . Two
> brothers, see? The Loman Brothers. . . .
> Baby, we could sell sporting goods!

Yet when it appears that Biff might actually get the money, even
though Happy makes some mention of getting money himself, Happy
is quite disturbed. He can brag to Stanley, the waiter, about
what a big man his brother is, but the compulsiveness with which

91

he goes about picking up a girl who walks into the restaurant reveals his anxiety. Just after Happy brags that he may be "going into business together with his brother," his attention is riveted to the girl who walks in.

> Happy, _raising his head_: Sh!
>
> Stanley: What?
>
> Happy: You notice I wasn't lookin' right or left, was I?
>
> Stanley: No.
>
> Happy: And my eyes are closed.
>
> Stanley: So, what's the--?
>
> Happy: Strudel's comin'.

Happy's attempt to pick up the girl is a function of his desperate need to prove to himself that he is a strong man who will not turn into a woman while "going into business" with his brother. The defense is perfect. He can build Biff up ("Great football player. . . . Biff is quarterback with the New York Giants") and at the same time show his superiority to Biff. He, Happy, can get girls. Biff cannot. Happy will act like the older brother. He will show Biff how it is done. He has the confidence. Biff doesn't. He asks Biff, "You want her?" When Biff says, "Oh, I could never make that," Happy points out,

> I remember the time that idea would never come into your head. Where's the old confidence, Biff?

When Biff tries to turn the conversation back to Oliver, Happy insists on keeping the conversation in an area where he feels superior to Biff:

> Wait a minute. I've got to see that old confidence again. Do you want her?

Even though Biff says he doesn't, Happy insists:

> I'm telling you. Watch this. _Turning to the girl_: Honey? _She turns to him_. Are you busy?

What makes Happy's whole ploy even sadder is that the girl is a prostitute.

Since Happy and Willy share so many characteristics it would not be surprising to find that Happy has made an unconscious identification with Willy. This would explain his concern that Biff help Willy. It is not Willy he is concerned about, but himself. The fantasy is: I need Biff's strength and love; since I am Willy, if Biff gives strength and love to Willy, I am getting his strength and love. There is another aspect to this identification. I have already suggested that Happy is not "happy"; rather he suffers from extreme anxiety. In this sense, also, he identifies with Willy. That is, he is concerned with Willy's emotional difficulties because he associates Willy's difficulties with his own. When he tells Biff that "I'm getting nervous about him [Willy], y'know, Biff?", he is really telling Biff that he is concerned about his own emotional state. He may say he's been wanting

> to talk to you about Dad for a long time,
> Biff. Something's--happening to him,

but it is really his own emotional confusion he has been desperate to communicate. Happy needs Biff's strength and love to pull himself out of his difficulties. Thus it bothers Happy that "you're not settled, that you're still kind of up in the air. . . ." Happy may say, "He [Willy] just wants you to make good, that's all", but it is Happy who needs Biff's success. It is Happy who thinks it would be a good idea "if you just got started." Happy can encourage his brother, "come on, Biff, let's buck him [Willy] up," but it is Happy who needs bucking up. Happy hopes that Biff will "give him a whirl," but it is Happy who wants the whirl. In the second act when Happy learns that Biff has failed with Oliver, he wants Biff to lie to Willy because he, Happy, cannot stand the truth. Biff is to "tell him something nice" because Happy wants to hear something nice. It is Happy who "is never so happy as when he's looking forward to something!" Therefore he can suggest to his father that Biff's experience at Oliver's was "Terrific, Pop," that "Sure, Pop, sure" Oliver gave him a warm welcome, that "damn right" it's amazing that Biff gets that kind of welcome after ten, twelve years, and that "Oh, I know" Oliver's a hard man to see. But when Biff insists on hurting Willy by telling him the truth, Happy tries to stop Biff and attempts to rationalize the pen stealing incident. Despite Biff's failure, Happy can assure himself that "He'll strike something, Pop," and "He's gonna be terrific, Pop!" Of course, he cannot have Biff and Willy fighting in the restaurant. Similarly Happy tries to stop the terrible struggle between Biff and Willy at the conclusion of the second act. At the end of that argument, when Biff falls into Willy's arms and expresses his love for Willy, Happy is "deeply moved." It is important that after that expression of love Happy puts "his arm around Linda," who is, of course, the wife of the man he has identified with, and can announce:

> I'm getting married Pop, don't you forget it.
> I'm changing everything. I'm gonna run that
> department before the year is up. You'll see,
> Mom. He kisses her.

The love that Biff has given to Willy has made him, Happy, feel strong and a man.

Yet, paradoxically, it is Happy's very identification with Willy which not only causes him to help his father, but also to reject him. Happy is certainly aware that Willy is on the brink of emotional disaster. In the bedroom scene with Biff he tries to tell Biff just that. Yet at other times in the play he tries to deny this knowledge. In the middle of Biff's long scene with Linda in the first act, Happy can tell Biff, "Just don't call him [Willy] crazy." When Linda tries to excuse Willy's irrational behavior to Biff by explaining that Willy is merely "exhausted," Happy can chime in, "Sure!" His reaction upon hearing that Willy has been attempting to commit suicide is anger. After Linda explains about the hose and the nipple in the basement, he can say, "angrily: That--jerk." When Linda claims that Willy's life is in Biff's hands, he is again angry: "to Biff: How do you like that damned fool!" We see this same anger manifest itself in the Requiem. Miller describes Happy as "deeply angered." Happy can claim, "He had no right to do that. There was no necessity for it." Happy's anger constitutes a denial of the knowledge that Willy is deeply disturbed. Happy must deny this knowledge, because he is actually attempting to deny the knowledge that he, Happy, is deeply disturbed. He is angered by Willy's self-destructive behavior since it brings to the surface the knowledge that he, Happy, is also attracted to suicide. Willy "had no right" to remind Happy of his own feelings. When the girl in the restaurant suggests that Happy at least tell his father that they are leaving, Happy denies any relationship with Willy, any identification with him: "He's just a guy."

Faced by the fact of Willy's suicide, Happy denies its horror by viewing Willy's death as part of a continuing, upward struggle. Happy will take over for Willy. He will show everybody that "Willy Loman did not die in vain." Willy had the only dream Happy can consider, "He fought it out here, and this is where I'm gonna win it for him."

Footnotes

Chapter I: Linda

[1] Although Nelson can argue that Linda, in fact, "is so absorbed in his [Willy's] welfare and is so unquestionably compliant with his values that her potential for saving him is minimal" [1970, p. 107].

[2] For example, Parker can say, "Linda is the most sympathetic character in the play. Her famous 'attention, attention must be paid' speech is terribly moving in the theatre, perhaps too moving" [1969, p. 106].

[3] John Mason Brown can say in his review for the Saturday Review of Literature, "Miss Dunnock is all heart, devotion, simplicity. She is unfooled and unfooling. She is the smiling, mothering, hardworked, good wife, the victim of her husband's budget. . . . If she is beyond whining or nagging, she is above self-pity. She is the marriage vow--'for better for worse, for richer for poorer, in sickness and health'-- made flesh; slight in body but strong of faith" [1949, p. 32].

[4] Bliquez is one of the few writers to have touched on this point: "But if in this marriage admiration does transcend love, then it follows that for Linda the superiority is more important than any marital equality. This is hero projection on her part. It is to insure this superiority that Linda does not support her husband where he is weak" [1968, p. 384].

Chapter II: Biff

[1]Shatzky, for one, thinks Biff's self-knowledge at the
end of the play incorporates a "fuzzy agrarian myth which is as
tenuous as the salesman's" [1973, p. 109].

[2]Mander is the only critic I have found who touches on the
point (although he does not develop it): "Here [the Boston
scene] is the root of Biff's hatred for his father and all
his subsequent failures: for it is implied that in his failures
Biff is unconsciously punishing his father. . . . [He] wanted
revenge rather than success" [1961, p. 150].

Chapter III: Willy

[1]Some critics, like Hagopian, go so far as to argue that
Willy is not even the protagonist: "Miller and his critics
are in error in seeing the central character in the play as
Willy Loman. The protagonist of a drama must be the one who
struggles most for understanding, who achieves the most
transforming insight and whose motives, decisions, and actions
most influence the total situation" [1963, p. 118].

[2]Lewis puts it a slightly different way: "Since he cannot
sell himself in life, he can at least sell himself in death.
It is his final act of selling, for he is worth more to his
family through his paid-up life insurance" [1962, p. 297].

[3]Consider Artaud's thoughts on his own possible suicide:
"If I commit suicide, it will not be to destroy myself but to
put myself back together again. Suicide will be for me only
one means of _violently_ _reconquering_ myself, of _brutally_ _invading_
my being. . ." [1965, p. 56. My emphasis].

SELECTED BIBLIOGRAPHY

Allison, Gordon. New York Herald Tribune, February 12, 1949,
p. 9.

Artaud, Antonin. Artaud Anthology. Ed. Jack Hirshman. San
Francisco, 1965.

Atkinson, Brooks. New York Times, February 11, 1949, p. 27.

Barnes, Howard. New York Herald Tribune, February 11, 1949,
p. 14.

Bliquez, Guerin. "Linda's Role in Death of a Salesman."
Modern Drama, 10 (1968), pp. 383–386.

Brown, John Mason. Saturday Review of Literature, 32 (1949),
pp. 30–32.

Clark, Eleanor. "Old Glamour, New Gloom." Partisan Review,
16 (1949), pp. 631–635.

Ganz, Arthur. "The Silence of Arthur Miller." Drama Survey,
3 (1963), pp. 226–231, 235–237.

Gassner, John. The Theatre in Our Times. New York, 1954.

Gibbs, Wolcott. The New Yorker, 24 (1949), pp. 54–56.

Hagopian, John V. "Arthur Miller: The Salesman's Two Cases."
Modern Drama, 6 (1963), pp. 405–410.

Hall, C. S. "A Cognitive Theory of Dream Symbols." Journal of
General Psychology, 48 (1953), pp. 169–186.

Hayman, Ronald. Arthur Miller. London, 1970.

Hynes, Joseph A. "Attention Must Be Paid." College English,
23 (1963), pp. 63–76.

Keppler, C. F. The Literature of the Second Self. Tucson, 1972.

Lewis, Allan. The Contemporary Theatre. New York, 1962.

97

Mander, John. The Writer and Commitment. London, 1961.

Nelson, Benjamin. Arthur Miller: Portrait of a Playwright.
    New York, 1970.

Ovesey, Lionel. "Pseudohomosexuality, The Paranoid Mechanism,
    and Paranoia." Psychiatry, 18 (1955), pp. 163-173.

Parker, Brian. "Point of View in Arthur Miller's Death of a
    Salesman." In Arthur Miller: A Collection of Critical
    Essays. Ed. Robert W. Corrigan, pp. 95-109, 1969.

Schneider, David E. "Play of Dreams." Theatre Arts, 33
    (1949), pp. 18-21.

Shatzky, Joel. "The 'Reactive Image' and Miller's Death of a
    Salesman." Players, 48 (1973), pp. 104-110.

Withim, Philip M. "Tragic Catharsis and the Resources of the
    Ego." The Psychoanalytic Review, 60 (1973), pp. 497-518.

Karl Harshbarger was graduated Summa Cum Laude and Phi Beta Kappa
from the University of Oregon in 1954, took his M. A. in The
Writing Seminars at The Johns Hopkins University in 1957, and
received his Ph. D. in theatre from Carnegie-Mellon University
in 1966. He has been a Gilman Fellow, a Mellon Fellow and an
R. C. A. - N. B. C. Fellow in Theatre. Mr. Harshbarger is
published in The Atlantic Monthly, The Tulane Drama Review,
The Pacific Spectator, Players Magazine and Hartford Studies in
Literature; and is currently completing his second book (on
Sophocles' Oedipus). Mr. Harshbarger has held various directing
posts and has numerous acting credits in TV, radio and film. He
teaches theatre at St. Mary's College of Maryland, and is married
with no children.